Letters to My Friends

A No Guarantees Guide to Awakening

by John C. Conley

Plus Enlightening Dialogues with
Baba Ram Jahn

Live Wire Press
Charlottesville, Virginia

Copyright©2007
John C. Conley

All rights reserved, including the right to reproduce
this work or any portion thereof in any form whatsoever,
without permission in writing from the author,
except for brief passages in connection with a review.

Cover art©1997, Patricia S. Adler
Cover photo©2007, Istockphoto.com
Font: Astaire Pro©1999-2007 MyFonts.com, Bergsland Design

Live Wire Press
Charlottesville, Virginia
www.livewirepress.net

Library of Congress Cataloging-in-Publication Data

Conley, John C.
  Letters to my friends : a no guarantees guide to awakening / by John C.
Conley ; plus enlightening dialogues with Baba Ram Jahn.
     p. cm.
  ISBN 978-0-9727531-4-2 (alk. paper)
  1. Spirituality. 2. Conley, John C. 3. Spiritual biography. 4. Conley, John
C.--Interviews. I. Title.
  BL624.C6623 2007
  204.092--dc22
  [B]
                                                        2007007181

ISBN 978-0-9727531-4-2

10 9 8 7 6 5 4 3 2

Printed in the United States

for

Joan

Dear Friends,

As I write these words, I am thinking about death. Perhaps these mutated cells called cancer are only visiting my body, and I will live many more years. Or, perhaps these cells plan to multiply and make a home here, and I will be dead within a short time. I do not know which it will be. As a friend once told me, "Some karma can be softened, and some can not." Why am I telling you this? Because if you are looking for easy answers or secrets, do not read this book. On the other hand, if you would enter deeper into Stillness, perhaps this book is for you.

As I read the letters in this book, I felt moved by the power in them. I felt strength and hope surge in me. I felt truly stunned that I had written them. But mostly I felt humbled. In reading these letters, I see that I am a wise man. Or to be more exact, I sometimes stumble over wisdom and fall so hard that even I recognize it! But I am also just John, confused, frightened, and sometimes bumbling.

As a young man, I was scarred by life; and that young man is in these letters. I was full of pain. I hurt everyone I loved. Lord knows I wanted to be a good man, but there was so much hurt and anger stored in me that no matter how much I tried to do the right thing, I would sabotage myself. I loved deeply, but my love was always mingled with a desperate need to be accepted. And invariably I drove away those I loved.

But now, as I enter more and more into what I call Stillness,

I feel somehow untouched by the hardships of my life. I feel young. I feel silly. I seek peace, but I am unafraid to speak my truth. I can love deeply with no expectation of anything in return. I am unpredictable. I am a little wild. I am intense, very intense. I love to hug and dance and sing. I am learning to treat myself with compassion, and as I do, I am healed. And as I am healed, my sense of Stillness deepens.

Of course, I still hurt myself and others. I do not claim to be enlightened. I get frightened. I want to be loved and I want it with a yearning so strong I still sometimes drive away those I love. But I am learning more and more to listen to the Stillness within me. And as I do, I find myself more and more in the flow of life. There, in that wild flow of Stillness, I find great joy. I hope you will join me in Stillness. I hope you will find great joy, and I hope these letters will help you do just that.

Blessings,
    John Conley

Spring

March 20

Dear Friends,

I have never been to the high mountains of Tibet to study Buddhism. I have never been to China to study the Tao. Nor have I been to Japan to study Zen or to India to study Hinduism. And never have I been to Jerusalem to study the mystic traditions of Judaism, Christianity, or Islam. I am not a scholar of the Bible, the Koran, or the Bhagavad-Gita. I have not written learned papers, nor am I ever likely to do so.

No angels have visited me. I do not have visions. I do not channel aliens or ancient entities. I am very, very average. Yet, just as do you, I carry with me always the ultimate secret of life, and that secret is what I call Stillness. Choose the name you desire. Stillness is my favorite. But I use God and Presence as well. But you may choose Higher Power, Krishna, Allah, or Jahweh. The name matters not so much as the experience behind the name.

We are all of us, humble and proud, knowledgeable and unknowledgeable, rich and poor, equal. For we are all born into Stillness, live in Stillness, and die in Stillness. That is all we need to know. But the knowing of it can take a lifetime because to know we need to listen, and to listen we need to be still.

Stillness is the universal force, the intelligence, the energy, that flows through and supports all of life.

Stillness is God. And God is Stillness. This is the circle of truth that infuses all religions. This circle of Stillness has been hidden from us, though. And only a few have seen it. It has been hidden in rituals and ceremonies and beliefs and faiths and dogmas. It has been hidden, not through any plan of evil, but only because people are people.

How can something so simple as Stillness be true? We must beautify it and amplify it. We must complicate it, for that is how we are. We need to disguise Stillness and make it grand. We need to make it difficult to obtain. And, God help us, we need to go to war about it and slaughter each other in a battle where the victor shouts, "God is with me!"

But for those of us who are simple seekers, there is no need for any of this. We carry Stillness with us as a mother carries her child, cradled in her arms. And Stillness carries us always. We are inseparable from Stillness. All we need to do is listen to the sweet, gentle voice of Stillness, beckoning us into itself.

And when we listen, what will we hear? What will Stillness say? Stillness will first speak to us through our feelings, our deepest feelings. Stillness will say *joy*. Stillness will say *forgiveness*, of ourselves, and of others. Stillness will say *compassion*. Stillness will say *rest*. Stillness will say *be at peace*. And above all, Stillness will say, "Be still and know that I am God." But Stillness will say this as an invitation, not as a threat.

Stillness will never say *hate*. Stillness will never say *hurt*. Stillness will never say *destroy*. So we listen. We listen for Stillness to speak to our feelings. How do we listen to our feelings? We hear our feelings with our heart. We feel joy in our heart. We feel forgiveness in our heart. But we also feel joy in our hands, in our arms and legs. Stillness speaks to us first through our bodies. This is so apparent, so simple, once we see it.

All meditations, all religions, all beliefs, faiths, and dogmas must lead us into this experience of Stillness. If they do not, they are a waste. Or at the very least, they are a sidetrack, a path leading into the brambles and the brush of endless intellectualism and sensationalism.

It is not that I have anything against the mind. I do not. I love to read. I love to learn new things and make new discoveries. I enjoy solving practical problems. But I know this beyond any doubt. We do not find God with our minds. We do not hear God with our minds. We do not know God with our minds. We find, hear, and know God with our hearts, with our bodies. Our minds are there only to interpret the experience. And here, of course, is where we all get into trouble.

Perhaps we experience Stillness on a mountain top while chanting. Perhaps we have a vision that an angel appears to us and tells us that we have found favor with God. Perhaps we believe this way, our way, is the only way. Perhaps we start a religion. Perhaps we start a war. The worst of the world's wars have been wars of religious supremacy. In other words, our minds can sabotage Stillness.

Almost without exception, the founders of the religions of the world have spoken messages of peace and compassion. Yet somehow we twist their truth. We turn a Jewish Prince of Peace into the God of War. We take an Indian monk and turn him into a God and then fight wars to spread the truth. So be careful of your mind. Be careful of my mind. Listen first and last to the Stillness in your heart, for that Stillness is God.

To know Stillness, all you need to do is go into Stillness. That is all. There is nothing more. Everything else arises from Stillness. Do you want peace of mind? Go into Stillness. Do you want to face life with courage? Then go into Stillness. Do you want more patience? Then go into Stillness. Do you want to be more compassionate and forgiving? Then go into Stillness. Do you want to be more creative? Then go into Stillness. Do you want more abundance in your life? Then go into Stillness. Do you want to be more accepting? Then go into Stillness.

All that you need, all that you seek is in Stillness. And Stillness flows through you now as a stream of energy that can be felt. This energy, which is Stillness, can be felt as joy in every fiber of your body. It can be felt as peace in every fiber of your body. It can be felt as Stillness in every fiber of your body. Turn your attention away from your busy mind and into this Stillness and you will know peace. Through this simple transfer of attention, this simple shift, Stillness will be your constant companion.

Perhaps some day together we will go to China and study the Tao. We will enjoy ourselves and absorb the wisdom of the ancients, but we will find nothing that is not ours now, in this moment. Perhaps someday we will study the ancient scriptures in Israel, and we will love the discoveries we make, but we will find nothing we do not have now, in this moment. For, wherever we go, we go in Stillness.

Rest in Stillness. Go in Stillness. Rest assured that all we need to know, to do, and to be will be revealed in its own time as Stillness unfolds through us and as we unfold Stillness.

Blessings,
    John Conley

John C. Conley

Questioner: Master, tell me about entering into Stillness.

Baba Ram Jahn: Well, my daughter, one can enter through the back door, or one can enter through the front door. But for three or four to enter, they must go single file. I suppose one could enter through the window, unless of course, the window was on the second floor, in which case one might fall. And, of course, sometimes windows get stuck shut, especially in old houses.

Questioner: Baba, you are so silly!

Baba Ram Jahn: Au contraire, my daughter. You asked me a serious question. Entering into the Silliness is very important. That is why I do it several times each day!

March 27

Dear Friends,

 I have heard many times that this form I call myself is an illusion and that as long as I remain in the illusion I will be reborn again and again. This illusion of form I call myself will die and someday turn into earth. My body of illusion will be food for bugs and worms, which will be eaten by birds, which will be eaten by foxes and cats. And the cats will end up sleeping on the beds of my children where they will be spoiled rotten.

 I must confess that I am firmly stuck in this illusion of form. Now, my children will dispute this. But perhaps the best I can hope for is that I will be reborn as one of my children. I will go to college and drive fast. I might wreck the car a few times and change my major in college several times. I might ask for money to travel to Europe, or money for a date. Being reincarnated as one of my children is sounding better all the time. I will get lots of foot rubs. I will be witty, charming, beautiful, and incredibly intelligent. I will have someone who always adores me and thinks I am special.

 But what if I do not reincarnate as one of my children? What if I change into a rock? Then what will I do? I might be buried under the ground. I will not be seen. And certainly I will not get my feet rubbed. I suppose I might get made into a sidewalk or a fireplace, but after the first few fires, how interesting would that be?

 Where am I going with this? Oh, yes, the illusion of form. Several years ago, I heard a teacher tell a woman with cancer that ultimately her illness did not matter because it was an illusion. This may have been true in some ultimate sense. But I have found that no matter how spiritual I think I am, I still think of myself as this form. I still think of myself as John with a body. And when my body hurts, I hurt.

So, all this teaching about not identifying with form really does not matter to me. It does not comfort me. It is a pretty intellectual construct, but it does not alleviate suffering. It is lifeless and sterile. In my darkest moments, in the wee hours of the morning, I admit to myself that I do not want to die. I do not want to suffer. I do not want to leave those I love. I want God to care for me. I do not care if I am not my form.

So what do I do? I turn to God, of course. I turn to a God I knew as a little boy. I always seem to be returning to the beliefs of my childhood. I believe God loves us. And it would be a really good thing if we loved each other, too. God would like that. And I believe that when I cry, God cries with me. And I believe that when I am afraid, God stands by me. These beliefs, however childish, give me comfort. And comfort is a good thing.

But in truth, I do not know the truth. God is mysterious, and I am ignorant. Perhaps I am not my form. So, years down the road, if you do see a cat yowling at night, please do not throw a rock at it. Not only is this unkind, but you might be throwing me at me.

Be rowdy,
    John Conley

Letters to My Friends

Baba Ram Jahn: Today, my dear daughter, I would like to talk about nonsense.

Questioner: Is talking about nonsense wise, Father? What if one had no sense about nonsense? Or what if one had some sense about no sense? Or, worse yet, what if one sensed nonsense in others but not in oneself? On the other hand, Father, remaining quiet about nonsense makes no sense, because no one with sense would know that you were thinking of talking about nonsense.

Baba Ram Jahn: What you say certainly makes sense to me, questioner.

Questioner: And that, Father, is why I love you!

April 3

Dear Friends,

When I close my eyes, I can see luminous strands of light stretching from me both forwards and backwards into eternity. These strands are my fate, and I know of only one way to free myself of them.

Who we think we are at any given moment in time is but one of the many strands that flow through our life. However, we make the mistake of believing only one strand defines our life. We grab onto this strand and cling to it. We call it life, and we believe that this strand is the only strand. We are blind to the many other strands that flow through us unseen and untouched.

For example, we may latch onto the strand we call anger. We may decide that is how we are, and how we always will be. Or, we may latch onto the victim strand, and we will allow nothing to shake us from our conviction that we are victims. These are the strands of our personal history.

Were we but able to see, we could change our entire life in a moment. We could be enlightened now. We could live lives of abundance now. Simply by grabbing onto the strands of our dreams. But we are blind, or at the very least, I am blind.

I know other strands are there, strands that will free me from my perception of myself. These are the strands of liberation, but I am unable to grasp them, unable, at times, to even believe they exist. Looking backwards, all strands lead to this point in time inevitably. Looking backwards, I had no choice in who I am or what I am or where I am. Everything in the entire universe conspired to put me in this moment at this time.

When I close my eyes, I see these strands, reaching backwards for billions of years and then stretching forward to this point. I see them vaguely as luminous strands of my karma. Is this vision real? I do not know. But it helps me grasp without words the enormous power that is behind me now, the forces that keep me locked in the prison of my perception.

Conversely, this vision also helps me understand intuitively the interconnectedness of us all. Truly, our smallest acts of kindness reverberate forever, as do our smallest acts of meanness. And were it not for the infinite goodness of the Universe, of God, I believe we would have long ago destroyed the world.

So, on one hand I know that in a limitless universe, both time and space cease to exist. What is even a billion years in infinity? It is nothing. It does not even exist. And what are a billion light years in an infinite universe? Nothing. In God, all things are at all times.

Yet, despite this knowledge, I know that time and space lead inexorably to this point in time. The entire universe has conspired for countless billions of years to bring us to this point of now. Perhaps this is another way of saying the universe is both infinitely personal and infinitely impersonal. Looking backwards, this point in time was inevitable. It could not exist in any other way. But looking forwards, nothing is set, if we live in Stillness.

For in Stillness we have the power to change our destiny. We have the power to grab another strand, which will lead us to realms unknown. And if we are not still, we are slaves of our past. We have no choice but to be who we are. Some of us are pleased with who we are. Others of us hate who we are. Some of us are biochemists and we win the Nobel Peace Prize. Some of us make drugs in the basement and sell them on the street. Some of us live in big houses and have servants. Others of us—most of us—are servants. In any case, unless we are still, we have no choice.

This is why many spiritual texts say that even the good among us will not enter the kingdom of God. This teaching is not a threat, nor are we being asked to be better people, or to be moralistic, upstanding people. It is a simple statement of fact. Our humanness is incomplete without the power of Stillness. And, if you believe as I do, Stillness is incomplete without our humanness.

So, what do we choose? Do we choose the safe slavery of the past? Or do we choose the unknown realms of Stillness. And here I mean emotional realms. I do not care if I can ever bend a spoon or travel through time and space in the blink of an eye. Doing so would be fun, but I doubt if it would lead me into Stillness. The unknown realms of which I speak are the ones referred to by Christ when he spoke of the peace that surpasses understanding. True miracles happen in the human soul. When a bitter old man finds peace after a lifetime of hard, boring work, leading to nothing but poverty, that is a miracle. When a young single mother, full of hatred directed toward her ex-husband, finds peace, that is a miracle. When the wife of a man with prostate cancer finds peace, that is a miracle. When the man with cancer finds peace that is a miracle. If in our future we explore faraway galaxies and make undreamed of discoveries, these achievements will pale alongside the miracle of inner peace.

And this peace is ours through Stillness. I obviously use the word Stillness much like many people use the word God. But Stillness is not something in which we believe. It is not something we worship or follow. Stillness is not a being that is separate from us. Stillness is not something we will ever understand intellectually no matter how many books we read and no matter how keen our minds.

Stillness is something we are. And it is something we do. To me, this is the cosmic joke. Stillness is so mundane and ordinary we miss it. I will never in a million years, fully understand Stillness, nor be able to explain it, no matter how much I read, no matter how long I go to school, no matter how much I discuss it with my friends. But I also know this, we, you and I, can enter Stillness now, in this moment.

By practicing Stillness, we sever the strands that bind us to our past, a past that determines our future. We sever these old strands through our decision to do so, and we gather new strands to ourselves.

Imagine yourself alone, floating in space. It is dark and your aloneness is vast. At your feet, flaring out in a canopy, you see the billions of strands of light, of energy, that have brought you to this time and place. These strands of luminous energy break through the darkness, stretching back to before the beginning of time. Some of these strands are very personal. Some are very impersonal. Some hold good memories. Some hold bad.

You lift your eyes and look up. There, stretching into the infinite future are the strands of your future. Your future is completely predictable. Everything you will do, everything others will do to you is fated to be by the strands of your past.

But, as you gaze about, you realize that everything that ever existed and everything that ever will exist is connected intimately with you. You see that everyone whoever existed, exists, or who will exist is equal in this universe. You see that if you move even your little finger, wiggle it just a bit, the whole universe wiggles.

And in this recognition of your connection to all things, and of your power in all things, you become still. With power, you wave your hand below you and the strands of your past fall away. You wave you hand above you and the strands of your future fall away, and in their place appear new strands. You gather these new strands to you and form them into a cord of Stillness that can never be broken. The power of the entire universe flows through you now—as it always has—through your mind, through your feelings, through your body. You see that you are a part of God and God is a part of you. You see that never before have you been more fully human. You are aware now. You are still now.

Thank you,
    John Conley

Questioner: I fell in love today, Master, with a boy.

Baba Ram Jahn: Tell me about it, my daughter.

Questioner: We walked together and gazed into each other's eyes. I felt so happy, Master. I have never felt that way before. I do not know what happened.

Baba Ram Jahn: Let me explain it, child, the divine spark in you responded to the divine spark in him. What you experienced was a divine meeting of souls. Do you understand?

Questioner: No, Master, when I look at you, I see the divine spark and I feel loved. But when I look at Sylvan, I see his divine brown eyes and his divine smile and I feel loved. You see, Master, he is very handsome.

Baba Ram Jahn: Well, my child, that is often the case. The divine spark pales in comparison to the divine face.

Questioner: Then is it not good, Master, that they are different aspects of the same thing? You have taught me well.

April 10

Dear Friends,

I remember my father used to admonish me, "Do one thing at a time, John. Even the longest journey only has one step, the one you are taking now." Or, if he felt exasperated he might say, "Would you pay attention!" Or, if he felt really, really exasperated, he might say, eyes bulging, "Jesus H. Christ." He was often a prayerful man in my presence. I never knew what the "H" stood for though, and I still do not.

Later in life I heard variations of my father's admonitions. *Live one day at time* is one of my favorites. And many teachers over the years have exhorted us to live in the now. I guess my father was a man before his time.

Yet, despite all these exhortations from my father and from other teachers, my experience has been the exact opposite. As a matter of fact, I would say my very survival depends on doing two things at once, on being two places at once. Or perhaps I should say my survival depends on being two things at once.

Possibly I am misinterpreting everything I have ever read, which bothers me not in the least. For, if I know one thing, it is that I know nothing for certain; and therefore I do not need to cling to my beliefs. The fact that I do cling to them, rather tenaciously at times, is irrelevant because, again, I do not need to cling to them. I do so only because I enjoy making myself and others miserable. If I do not control the world, who will?

I am getting off track here. My train has jumped the track and is careening its way through the adjacent forest. From the pines and firs, from the oaks and maples, birds fly upwards to escape the rushing train, and as they fly, they squawk, "Who is this man? Doesn't he know enough to keep his train on the track?"

Well, actually, I do. But staying on the track all the time can be so boring. Tracks are fine unless we allow them to rule our life. And why should we? For truly, we can know nothing for certain. So why stay on track with what we do not know? Why not risk being wrong, being silly, being misdirected and misguided? Let us relish and revel in our ignorance, for in the end that is all we have.

How can we know anything? I know I am sitting on a flat world and the sun revolves around the world. We all know this. It is obvious. Ask anyone. Yes, I know that scientists say the world is round and the earth revolves around the sun. But my senses tell me the scientists are wrong. Not only that, the scientists interpret their data with the same five senses with which I interpret my existence. If I cannot trust my senses and the interpretation of my mind on such a simple matter as which ball revolves around which ball, how can I trust my senses and my mind on the infinitely more complicated matter of Stillness? I cannot, for I can know nothing for certain. Am I back on track yet? I do not know!

My ignorance is not a bad thing. Rather, it points me into Stillness, a state of being that I cannot explain. Nor do I know if Stillness truly exists. How could I, or anyone else, possibly know such a thing? In my world, God is very, very big.

And if I can know nothing for certain, does that mean I am lost? Yes, it probably does. Therefore, I choose to be lost in Stillness. If I cannot know reality, then at the least I can make my reality a pleasant one. And Stillness is the most pleasant thing I have found. It is full of joy and laughter. It does not care about knowing or not knowing. I love being lost in Stillness. In Stillness, my need to be serious, my need to be right, my need to be lucid and coherent diminishes almost to nothing. Frightening, isn't it?

So, back on track, let us be reasonable and not dilly-dally in the realms of the unknowable. I need to do two things at once and I will always need to do two things at once. For if I do not, I will be lost in places I would rather not be. The longest journey begins with two steps.

I need to live in this flat world. And I need to live in Stillness. I need to feed my children. I need to live in Stillness. I need to work. I need to live in Stillness. I need to be a blessing to all whom I meet. I need to live in Stillness.

When I am angry, I need to be also still. When I am afraid, I need to be also still. When I am alone, tired, and sick, I need to be also still. I choose the unknowing of Stillness. I live in two worlds, neither of which I can know are real. Or perhaps I live in two manifestations of one world, neither of which I can know are real.

Ultimately, I do not think it matters whether they are real or not. So where does this leave us? In this I turn to my best friend. She teaches little children, and in speaking to her I realize that in many ways people do not change. What works for children will work for us. So here are the rules I live by, rules I believe to be real.

Be nice. Don't shove. Don't call people names. Have fun. Laugh and run. Jump in mud puddles. Be still. And above all, if you ever say Jesus H. Christ to a little one, please explain what the "H" means. I mean, really, what does the "H" stand for? Jesus Halleluiah Christ? Jesus Help Christ? Jesus Holy Christ? Jesus "Have I told him a thousand times not to do that and I am losing my patience" Christ? I think it was probably the last one.

Blessings,
    John Conley

Questioner: What is your favorite meditation, Master?

Baba Ram Jahn: My favorite meditation is to stand on my head and shout "I am enlightened. I am enlightened. I am enlightened." I say this thirty-six times while facing the rising sun at midnight. And I hold my breath while I shout, all the while visualizing a red light descending from my first chakra to my sixth chakra and exiting through my ears in a counter clockwise spiral. In truth, though, I have not progressed as far as I would have wished with this meditation.

Questioner: But Master, that is ridiculous! How could this ever lead you to Nirvana? For one thing, the sun does not rise at midnight!

Baba Ram Jahn: So that is what I am doing wrong!

April 17

Dear Friends,

Dannie is her name. She is eleven and for one night she was my teacher. I needed a break from talking. About twelve of us, many of them strangers to me, laughed and told stories in the spacious living room of Dannie's house. But sorrow lurked there. Nathan had severe memory loss and could not follow the conversation, at least not our conversation. His wife, May, served him. "Would you like a little more salad?" May asked. Her husband frowned at her. "I think we should put more wood on the fire."

There was no wood, no fire, and no need for either. The heat of one those warm winter days we had been having still clung to the evening air. May smiled and laughed, but if you looked closely, you could see the sorrow flit across her face hummingbird quick. "I think you're right, Nathan. Just as soon as we eat."

And in the next room, Nathan's brother, Henry, rested as he had been doing for weeks. Henry is Dannie's great uncle. And Nathan is her grandfather. Dannie's mother and father had welcomed Henry into their home while he fought one of the biggest battles of his life.

Cancer had its claws in Henry, slowly devouring him bite by bite. But Henry fought back. He had been raised in a little town called Lebanon. The men there were loggers, farmers, mill workers, and merchants. Many of them drank hard and fought hard. And not a quitter lived among them. And after a twelve-hour shift, after they threw their last punch and drank their last beer on a Saturday night, they slept it off and the women, twice as tough as the men, dragged the men and kids to church on Sunday morning. In church, men like Reverend Reep told everyone about the wages of sin, as if they needed reminding.

This little town of Lebanon, that's where I grew up too. And Reverend Reep was my minister. He never really had his heart into his fire and brimstone sermons, but what else was he to do with so many drunks and toughs? The women in Lebanon wanted fire and brimstone, or so my father claimed. He said that the women wanted all the rotten husbands to burn in hell, maybe not for eternity, but long enough to teach them a lesson.

So, I felt no surprise when tough Henry tottered out of his bedroom supported by his wife. He told a few jokes and told a few stories from his boyhood. One of his best friends later became my high school principal. His job was to give direction. My job was to rebel. We did not get along. But that is another story.

After the jokes and stories, skinny as a beanpole, and supported by his wife, another smiling, tough woman, with pain on her face, Henry wove back to his bedroom for some sort of awful drug treatment.

Yes, I needed a break. Quite frankly, I no longer felt able to stay centered amidst so much pain. I am not very good at blocking pain. So, I said to Dannie, "Hey, let's shoot a few hoops." A little about Dannie. She is eleven, she is blond, she stands about five feet tall. And she should work in Las Vegas fleecing the innocent out of their money. We shot a few hoops. She missed every single one. "I'm not very good," she would say after every miss. "No, that's not true," I would reply, "You just need to practice."

Eventually, after nine or so more misses, I knew I could take her. With my best casual air, I said, "How about a game of HORSE?"

"Sure," she said, perhaps a little too quickly, a little too eagerly. For those of you who do not know, the game of HORSE is played as follows. One player shoots and if he or she makes the basket, the next player has to make the same shot. If the second player misses the shot, he or she gets a letter. The first player to spell HORSE loses.

I consciously practiced Stillness. I could feel the Stillness deep within. I was detached from the outcome of the game. Win or lose, I was one with the cosmos. Let us not string out the misery of this game too long, for I am a merciful man, and do not relish writing about the humiliation of defeat. Truly, what chance did an eleven-year old girl stand against a man who had meditated daily for years?

Let me put it this way, when I had HORS and Dannie had H, I knew it was time for me and the cosmos to get serious. On my last shot of the game, on the make it or break it shot, I looked at Dannie and said, "The ball wants to go into the net. The only thing between the net and the ball is my mind." Swoosh! I made it. Then Dannie took her next shot. "The ball wants to go into the net. Nothing stands between me and the net. My mind wants the ball to go into the net." Swoosh! She made it.

I was stunned. She had one upped me in the spiritual aphorism department. I instantly went into a spiritual reverie. Dannie made her next shot. I missed mine and lost the game. Honestly, had I not been in a spiritual reverie, I would have trounced her, beaten her into the ground, and destroyed all vestiges of her self-esteem. Not that I am competitive or anything. I would have trounced her in a very loving sort of way. I would have told her, "Now, Dannie, as the realization of your inevitable defeat crosses your mind, just watch the thought, nothing more. Be one with it."

It was that spiritual reverie. That is why I lost. "The ball wants to go into the net. Nothing stands between me and the net." In my reverie, Dannie's voice whispered, "My mind wants the ball to go into the net."

That has been my experience with practicing Stillness. My mind does want me to be still. My mind is evolving into Stillness and welcomes Stillness. And the part of my mind that welcomes Stillness gets stronger each time I practice Stillness.

This part of my mind is not harsh or judgmental. It does not browbeat me. It nudges me gently. When I get frightened or angry, this part of my mind says, "Remember Stillness?"

I have never been able to relate to teachings that turn us into our own worst enemies by vilifying our minds and feelings. These teachings typically spend an inordinate amount of time and energy trashing the ego and detailing the awful mental and emotional paths down which we will tread if we trust our minds.

Yes, of course, our minds can sabotage us. Is this news? But our minds can also be our friends on the spiritual path. Just ask Dannie, "The ball wants to go into the net. Nothing stands between me and the net. My mind wants the ball to go into the net."

Yes, Dannie is an insightful little girl, and tough too. This toughness seems to run in her family. I wonder if she was born in Lebanon? If so, all those bar room brawlers and gamblers back home better hang onto their money. "I'm not very good," she will tell them, as she whispers, "The ball wants to go into the net. Nothing stands between me and the net. My mind wants the ball to go into the net."

Blessings,
    John Conley

Letters to My Friends

Questioner: Master, why are basketballs always round?

Baba Ram Jahn: It is their karma. Once they learn all there is to know about being a basketball, they will be reborn as a football or baseball.

Questioner: But Master, karma does not tell me why the basketball is round! It only tells me that it is round.

Baba Ram Jahn: Ah, so you have noticed that too? I think you are turning into a spiritual skeptic, daughter. You really must watch the company you keep. Some things must be taken on faith. Follow my example, questioner.

April 24

Dear Friends,

Here is a little story that I would rather not tell, but I will. A few months ago, in downtown Portland, I sat in Yamhill Market. As I read the paper and ate my noodles and green beans, a huge woman, each of her legs as big as my waist, trudged toward the counter to order her food. She looked neither right nor left, but cast her eyes down. I imagine she did not want to see the eyes, mine and others, staring at her, judging her. Two teenage girls, both thin, sat at a corner table. They looked at her and laughed, covering their mouths with their hands.

I felt anger. I wanted to scold the girls. How could they be so cruel? Was it so hard to be compassionate? The lady did not so much breathe, as gasp, when she reached the counter. She gripped the edge of the counter to support herself. I felt pity. How hard her life must be. How difficult it must be to endure the glances, or worse yet, the giggles. And how hard it must be to endure the well-meaning advice from friends and family.

And then awareness of other emotions seeped into my consciousness. I felt loathing, disgust, contempt. How could she allow that to happen to herself? Was she too lazy to walk? Had she ever heard of eating less?

God, she is so fat.

And then a nasty little voice whispered to me, "If God made her fat, he made you shallow." Now I directed the loathing, disgust, and contempt at myself. How could I be so shallow? I was no better than the two girls. I was worse than them, for I judged both the girls and the woman. Who was I to judge? How could I possibly think these thoughts and feel these feelings and call myself a spiritual person? I was a fake.

And then a funny thing happened on the way to the familiar city of guilt and remorse. I became aware of the stream of these thoughts and feelings. And I was aware of a quietness underneath these streams. I was aware of the bedrock of the stream, the solid ground over which my thoughts and feelings hurled their way into the habitual patterns of my life. It was as though I was watching myself acting in a play, one in which I had acted many times before, and one in which I would act again.

In that moment, as I took a deep breath, I felt a subtle feeling of joy and aliveness in my body. This sense of aliveness grounded me in the inner quietness. And from that quietness, a wiser me spoke. "She is more than her body. The girls are more than their blindness. And you are more than your thoughts, more than your feelings."

"Yes," I said to my wiser self, "but how could I be so judgmental?"

To which my wiser self answered, "To be human is to judge and to judge is to find that which is judged lacking. It is the struggle that gives these thoughts power. Stop the struggle and the thoughts will return to the nothingness from which they came."

My wiser self continued, "If you think you should not think this or feel that, you will continue the struggle forever. Let go of your expectations and go into the quietness. Let your thoughts do what they will. But do not judge yourself. For these thoughts and feelings are those of a hurt and frightened man, and he, as do all beings, needs your love."

The discussion with myself ended. I sat for a few moments

longer in this Stillness. My surroundings, my awareness of my surroundings, they were somehow softer, not as threatening or as confusing. I knew that in a world where this sort of peace was possible, despite all the evidence to the contrary, that ultimately I lived in a good world.

In this quiet place, all my questions seemed like a game, fun but ultimately not important. In that Stillness, my questions about the nature of reality remained unanswered. I ceased to worry about why evil existed. I knew that the answer for every question was this peace and only this peace.

I will never be able to lucidly compare Tibetan Buddhism with Zen Buddhism. Nor will I ever be able to eloquently expound on the discourse between Arjuna and Krishna in the chariot before the battle. I will not be able to explain why so many people suffer so much. Or why I judge them when they do.

But I will be able to say that as we focus our awareness on this quiet place within us, our lives will slowly and implacably change for the better. We will experience more joy and peace, regardless of our circumstances. I cannot promise us an easy life, one where nothing ever goes wrong. But I can say this. Underlying all of reality, there is a field of peace, from which we can nourish ourselves whenever we so choose. And from that place we will make wiser choices and we will be a blessing to all whom we meet.

The lady got her food and shuffled to a table. I still felt sad for her. My judgment of her was now nothing more than a dim echo slowly being absorbed in the canyon of my Stillness. I got up to leave and silently thanked the lady for the lessons she had taught me. She had been a gift from God. As I left the Market, I glanced at the two girls. They were picking at their food, toying with it. A copy of a popular fashion magazine lay open on the table before them. They

Letters to My Friends

too were in a dance not of their own making. They too were gifts from God.

Blessings,
    John Conley

Questioner: Why, Baba Ram Jahn, would a Teacher ask, "What is the sound of one hand clapping?" I think this is so silly. Why not ask, "What is the sound of no hands clapping?" Or, "What is the sound of one fish flopping?" Or why not ask, "What is the taste of two eyes seeing?"

Baba Ram Jahn: Child, that is a wonderful koan. Magnificent. And what, daughter of my heart, do you think is the answer?

Questioner: Master, I make these things up. "What is the taste of two eyes seeing?" I have no idea what that means! But if I did know, I would say Stillness; for dear Father, I know that is what you would say!

Baba Ram Jahn: No, no, daughter, you misunderstood me. I liked, "What is the sound of one fish flopping?" It is the best koan ever! Where are the poles? Let's go find out!

May 1

Dear Friends,

One of the cornerstones of my spiritual practice is not knowing, for it is through not knowing that I am able to rewrite my past, and in rewriting my past, I rewrite my present, and in rewriting my present, I rewrite my future. If I know, if I am absolutely certain that what I know is right, then I block all that which I do not know from being born.

To know and to know unwaveringly is to be arrogant. If I know that mindfulness meditation is the right way to meditate, I block all other meditations, some of which are beautiful and would lift me up as the song of a robin in the early morning. If I know that my religion is the truth, then I block all the sweet teachings from all the other teachers. If, for example, I believe Jesus and only Jesus spoke the truth, then I do not listen to Buddha, or Krishna.

If I know that during meditation I should have no thoughts, then I discount all meditations where my thoughts continue. If I know that the present moment is the only moment in which I should dwell, then I block the rich history of my past and the rich history of my future.

It is better not to know, for then I am open to all the riches of the universe. I greet life and its teachings as a gift, not as an enemy, not as something to be conquered and destroyed. When I do not know, I live with an open heart. When I do not know, I allow life to flow through me. I allow my experience to be perfect and good because I am not constantly judging it and finding it wanting.

If I do not know, then I can do something that only a few of us are graced to do. I can rewrite my life. I can, perhaps, just perhaps, finally rewrite my past and escape from the chains that bind me. And this in turn allows me to live in the moment, fully embracing it. And living in the moment allows me to rewrite my future. For make no mistake, if we are bogged down in the swamp of knowing, our future has already been written. What we know today dictates how we live tomorrow.

So, in my not knowing, I believe the impossible is possible. Let me tell you a story. When I was a little boy, I had a teacher who was troubled, very troubled. One day she grabbed me by the hair and shook me. She screamed at me and said I was stupid. I can still see her brown eyes glaring at me with loathing. She slapped my face. I can still feel the shock as though it were yesterday. I was six at the most. There was nothing, absolutely nothing I could have done to deserve such treatment.

For many years, I resented her. I hated her. I knew she was evil and should be punished. Only recently did I forgive her. I went into my past and I took up my pen and set it to the paper of my life and wrote a new chapter in the book that is me. I wrote a page that said my teacher had been a vessel through whom God wanted to shine. But mud filled this vessel and through it God could not shine. Why had her vessel filled with mud? Who put it there? When she was six, who had glared at her with hatred? I began to forgive her. That God loved her and wanted to flow through her now seemed apparent to me.

But even with my new found insight, the pain of that distant day was there as though she had slapped me but a moment ago. The gorge of hate would rise up in me, and I would feel bitter and alone.

In my desire to be free of my own bitterness, I took a step into not knowing. I took a drastic step. In the Stillness of my heart,

I created a new vessel, a new teacher, one who did not need forgiveness. This teacher was kind and gentle. Her vessel had never been filled with mud. She loved me. She played with me. I think I was her favorite student.

Yes, I literally began to rewrite my past. I did not hang on to knowing my past as though it was written in a tablet of stone. I set myself free. That old teacher was, after all, only a memory, a thought that had lodged itself in my mind. And the new teacher, she is also a thought. Or is she?

How do I know I cannot literally rewrite my past? My loving first grade teacher makes me feel so much happier today. I feel almost as though this loving teacher really did exist and that I somehow got trapped in the wrong memory. I lived in the wrong memory. Now, of course, my rational mind will always remember that old teacher. I am not slipping into delusion. Or was my mean teacher the delusion?

How far will I go with this? How much of my history can I rewrite? I do not know. If I rewrite my past and turn my sorrows into joy, does that mean I am insane? Perhaps it is God who wants me to rewrite my past. Perhaps it is God who wants to free me from what I know. Can God be that big? Can God be that strange? Oh, I hope so. I really, really hope so. For, if this is insanity, and in my insanity I find love and forgiveness, then so be it.

Blessings,
John Conley

Letters to My Friends

Questioner: I have decided that the koan, "What is the sound of one hand clapping?" is very egotistical.

Baba Ram Jahn: And why is that?

Questioner: When the hand moves, it displaces air and this air moves in waves at 761 miles per hour at sea level. If the waves hit some blades of grass, the grass senses the wave. In other words, the grass moves. Who are we to say what constitutes hearing and what does not? How do we know the grass does not "hear" the sound of one hand clapping?

Baba Ram Jahn: So, when the wind blows, and the grass waves and the tree branches wave, they are all talking to each other? How delightful. I wonder what they are saying?

Questioner: Well, of course, Father, they are saying goodbye. Otherwise, why would they be waving?

May 8

Dear Friends,

There is just this and nothing more—Stillness. And above this Stillness plays the drama of my life. Troubles come and go. Dreams come and go. Suffering comes and goes. Happiness comes and goes. But under this drama, at all times, is the Stillness.

No words can substitute for it. I could read every book ever written about the spiritual path, understand them all, and yet I would not be one step, one word, closer to the Stillness. I could teach in great universities and not come any closer to Stillness.

I could write great books and be admired by millions and yet not be one step, one word, closer to Stillness. No, Stillness, the experience of our authentic self, is not to be found in words, not if we read those words only with our minds.

Nor can any teacher lead me into Stillness. If Christ were to appear before me and share his teachings of life with me, my understanding would not take me one step closer to Stillness. Buddha and Mohammed could join Jesus and expound on the all the secrets of the spiritual path, and my understanding would not take me one step closer to Stillness.

If my favorite teacher invited me to dinner and befriended me, explaining all knowledge to me, my understanding would not take me one step closer to Stillness. No, Stillness is not to be found in any teacher, no matter how profound and insightful, not if we listen only with our minds.

Nor, will good works lead me into Stillness. If I were to give of my wealth unstintingly, and serve the poor and the destitute the rest of my life, my generosity, no matter how noble would not lead me into Stillness. If I were to establish world peace, that would not lead me into Stillness. If I were to save the environment, that would not lead me into Stillness. If I were to save the cultures of the indigenous peoples of the world, that would not lead me into Stillness. Understanding, learning, generosity, these are all good things, wonderful things, but they will not lead me into Stillness, not if I approach them only with my mind. I must also listen with my heart. In other words, to find Stillness, I must first be still.

Where, then, does that leave us? Right where we have always been. Here, now, alone with ourselves, that is where it leaves us. And that is where Stillness is to be found. In us and only in us will we find Stillness. There is nothing more we need to do or understand. Stillness is who we are. We are Stillness and Stillness is us. We are connected with the universe in this moment. There is nothing, absolutely nothing, we can do to break that connection. And there is nothing, absolutely nothing, we can do to make it stronger.

All we need to do is quiet our minds and listen. That is all! Nothing more. Stillness is to be sensed with a quiet mind and an open heart. Here and now. So, yes, of course, the question is, "How do we quiet our minds?"

We could retreat to a monastery for twenty years and count our breaths or chant. But who would watch our children? We could find a cave and live in it until we either went insane or found the Stillness within. But who would care for our elderly? No, we cannot retreat. Not us, for we do not choose to shed our responsibilities. So, again, where does that leave us? It leaves us alone, here, now, with nothing but ourselves and that is all we need.

Do this now and you will touch the Stillness within yourself. Simply remember a time of joy in your life. It could be anything, from the mundane to the sublime. Now shift the focus of your mind from your thoughts to this feeling of joy and ask yourself how joy feels in your hands, your face, your throat, your chest and stomach, your legs, and feet. Feel the joy in your body. Breathe now through every cell of your body. How does joy feel? Now, gently look under the felt sense of joy and you will see Stillness. Rest there. If your thoughts are racing, fine. Bring yourself back to your felt sense of joy and follow it into Stillness.

Stillness is always enlivening every fiber of our bodies. And our bodies embrace the Stillness. Our bodies, no matter how tired, no matter how healthy or how ill, simply purr in the joy of Stillness. And that is why this meditation of joy is so powerful.

This is so simple, so easy, that is seems impossible to believe that it would work. But it does because we quit resisting our minds and focus on the felt sense of aliveness in our bodies, and in doing so, joy arises as the morning sun. However, even though it is easy and simple, it paradoxically takes vigilance, commitment, and discipline, especially at first. It takes vigilance because we become so easily lost in our minds. It takes commitment because, especially at first, we will not believe this simple practice works. And it takes discipline because, even after we believe it works, our tendency will be to fall back into our old ways.

But there will be a day when we become like runners who run for the joy of it. We will be still for the joy of it. And on that day, if Jesus, or Buddha, or Mohammed were to appear before us in the flesh, we could join them in Stillness. We could hear them and understand them. We could become fully human and fully divine. It is so very simple.

Thank you,
    John Conley

Letters to My Friends

Questioner: Master, I just read that the Dalai Lama is the Divine Head of Tibetan Buddhism. Why do so many Buddhists have troubles with their bodies?

Baba Ram Jahn: I am not sure what you mean, questioner.

Questioner: First, from the famous Zen koan, we have the sound of one hand clapping and now we have the Divine Head. Where is the rest of his body? Is it at home asleep? Should I call a doctor? What if some corporate headhunters find him? He will not be able to run. Why couldn't he be the Divine Body? Perhaps then he could get a head.

Baba Ram Jahn: I am not sure how to answer that, child. But I do not think he could be the Divine Body. After all, he has already lost his hand!

May 15

Dear Friends,

    Does your mind want perfection? Mine does. Now our image of perfection may vary, but I believe we all want perfection. One of us wants the perfect mate, a beach house on Maui, perfect children with perfect grades, and perfect white teeth. Another of us may want spiritual enlightenment. We want to live in a state of bliss as life passes in front of us leaving us untouched. Yet another one of us may want perfect freedom, the freedom to do want we want, when we want, and how we want.

    However, most of us want. Like an adventurous cook creating a new dish with a little bit of this and a little bit of that, we might say to ourselves, "I will take the house on Maui, the perfect mate, a touch of enlightenment, and a dash of freedom." And when we take our creation out of the oven of life, we might say to ourselves, "Voilà, the perfect life."

    And at first, as we take the perfect dish from the oven, we might even believe ourselves, at least until we taste our creation. Then a friend will get AIDS. A daughter will take drugs. We will get cancer. A loved one will die. We will get stuck in traffic. Our son will drop out of college. A beloved pet will get hit by a truck. We will get fired. We will have more bills than money. We will take the perfect creation of our life out of the oven, and it will taste bitter, as though the gods above dropped bile on it. And as we taste the bile, we will realize that life does what it wants, when it wants, and how it wants, seemingly with no concern whatsoever with what we want.

    And this revelation may be the most important fork in the

road of our life. We can go on as before. We can try harder to create a perfect life. We can read more books. We can attend classes on abundance. We can attend seminars on awakening. We can do all of these things. We can do them the rest of our lives. No one will stop us. And if we are fortunate we may even gain some temporary relief from our pain. Yes, pain.

It is pain, and nothing more, that fuels our highest aspirations, even the aspiration to become enlightened. Pain that drives us to try harder and harder until we want to quit, until we want to hide. Until, for some of us, we want to die because the pain consumes us like an everlasting fire. We wake up one morning after all our striving and we understand we are in hell.

And it is at this moment, if we but turn to it, that we will find the Stillness. We can wade into Stillness as though it were a gentle river flowing through the desert of pain. We can allow this river to ease our pain and wash it away. Jesus spoke of this Stillness as though it were a father, a father who holds, loves, and comforts his hurt and frightened child. One has but to experience this Stillness once to understand why Buddha spoke of it as bliss. This Stillness heals our hearts and soothes our fears. It calms our minds. This Stillness can be felt as joy in every fiber of our being.

The concept of a universal, intelligent God is literally beyond my comprehension. I may think I know, but I do not. But Stillness is not beyond my comprehension. Joy is not beyond my comprehension. Peace is not beyond my comprehension. I feel these.

And here is the most amazing thing of all: I can feel this Stillness even when my life is not perfect. I can feel this Stillness when I am sick. I can feel this Stillness when I fear poverty. This Stillness cannot be frightened away by the noise of my life. This is why Christ said, "I am with you always." He had become that

Stillness so much so that he knew that there was no division between himself and it. This is why he said, "I and the Father are one." And now today, we can say, Stillness is in me and I am in it.

This Stillness is a healing breath. Does your loved one hurt? Close your eyes now. Breathe deeply. Breathe slowly. Be comfortable. Now imagine your loved one with all her pain, all her sorrow standing before you. Breathe in her pain deeply and slowly. Hold her pain in the Stillness at the end of the in breath. Now, as you breathe out, surround your beloved in light—radiant, bright light. Send it through your eyes. Send it through your heart. Send it through every fiber of your being.

Again, breathe in the pain and sorrow of your loved one. Notice your own pain and sorrow rising to meet that of your loved one. You see resentment. You see disappointment. Anger. Perhaps you even see loathing or hate. It is nothing compared to the Stillness. Breathe all the pain, yours too, into the Stillness at the end of the breath. Now, again, breathe out light—healing, radiant light to your loved one.

Keep doing this, and you will feel the Stillness deepen in your heart. You will grow calm as your heart, mind, and body meld into the Stillness. Now, instead of breathing in the sorrow of your loved one, see her radiating light back to you and see yourself breathing in the light she sends. Now sit in Stillness, healing and being healed, as long as is comfortable.

This meditation is one of the most powerful I know. It can turn my pain into joy, even when the outward circumstances of my life are not all that I would like. This meditation is ancient, probably more ancient than I know. I read that a Buddhist monk first taught a version of it a thousand years ago. But I imagine he may have heard it from someone else who heard it from someone else who

Letters to My Friends

heard it from Stillness. Make it your own and you will come to know that even though you may have but little control over your life, you have control of your heart's response to life.

Thank you,
    John Conley

Questioner: I think that Catholics and Buddhists are very much alike, Master.

Baba Ram Jahn: And why is that, child?

Questioner: Well, the Dalai Lama is the Divine Head of Tibetan Buddhism, and I just read that the Pope is the Holy See of the Catholic Church. Why not the Holy Hearer? Or the Holy Taster? Or the Holy Smeller? Would this not be a more complete Pope?
    I think the Pope is a wonderful man and I am going to send him a letter about my concerns. As a matter of fact, I think he should get together with the Dalai Lama and discuss having a whole body.

Baba Ram Jahn: That, my daughter, would be a very wise suggestion. I am sure he will appreciate it.

May 22

Dear Friends

I remember a little girl named Alice. I remember her hair was red and curly and cut short. She wore big pinkish glasses perched on a pug nose. She smiled all the time and laughed easily. Freckles dotted her face. I thought she was cute, but much too young for me. I think she was in the fifth grade, and I was in the sixth.

She had one complete arm. Her left arm ended just above the elbow. She had been born that way. One day, on the playground, near that huge Douglas fir near the muddy softball field, I saw a group of boys, and I heard a girl crying. Something compelled me to move toward the tree and the boys and the crying. When I got there, I saw Alice, her back against the tree, as she faced the boys. Her one hand covered her eyes and she wept noisily. Before her stood Billy. He laughed and said, "How does it feel to be an ugly, little cripple?" The other boys laughed.

I walked up behind Billy, jerked him around, and said, "Stop it!"

He laughed at me and I hit him in the face with my face. He fell backward onto the ground and I jumped on him and began smashing his face as hard and fast as I could. Blood spurted everywhere. Billy cried and struggled to get away, but he could not. Nor could I leave. Even as a sickness spread through me, I did not seem able to stop. Two other boys jumped on me. I shrugged them off. I kept hitting Billy. Then I heard a voice yelling, "Stop it! Stop it! You'll kill him! Stop it!" I felt a little hand tug at my shirt. Alice leaned her tear stained face close to me. "Please stop it. You're hurting him."

The rage fled from me. I barely had the strength to get up. I looked at the shock on the faces around me and walked away from all of them. I never said a word to Alice after that incident, not one. Every time I saw her, I remembered that sick feeling of horror as I smashed Billy's face.

So, you tell me. Did I do the right thing in helping her? You might say I could have reasoned with Billy to stop. But I would tell you that he would never have stopped. Billy was a bully. He took joy in tormenting the weak and helpless. He had no reason to fear me. I shunned fights. And I will tell you something else. He never bothered Alice again. So, you tell me. Did I do the right thing? Did I act out of compassion? I wanted to save Alice. I wanted to protect her. Did I do the loving thing?

Years later, I overheard my mother talking to a friend from church about Billy and his family. Billy's father was a drunk. He beat Billy's mother. And he beat Billy. That was the long and short of the conversation. I registered it and refused to think about it. I refused to feel anything about it.

But just a few days ago, Billy came back as I was quietly meditating. I felt full of peace and joy. And then Billy joined me. He, looking lonely and confused, stood in my mind. I went back to my breath, and then Alice showed up. And I felt sick, really, really sick. In my memory, I saw little Alice. I saw Billy teasing her. I saw me punching Billy's face. I saw Alice trying to stop me. I saw Billy's father beating him. And into the quietness of my own soul, I said, "What else could I have done?"

We can talk about Stillness and love all day long and all night long. We can read all sorts of books and meditate twelve times each day. We can have mystical experiences, talk to angels, see God, and be one with everything. And then, when you least expect it, you're faced with one of those moments that will define you forever. And it all comes down to this. What are you going to do? Are you going to stand by? Are you going to get involved? Are you going to fight? What is the right thing to do?

Billy, if you're out there, I am really sorry. I feel terrible for hurting you. I really do. You were just a kid. You had a rotten father. I would like to think he loved you, but he was a drunk and didn't know how to show his love. I'm sorry he beat you. I'm sorry you turned out the way you did.

My father wanted me to save the world. He never said it that way. But that is exactly what he wanted. It's been a burden at times. I'm not much of hero. And honestly, ever since that day I pounded your face, I've been afraid of myself. I didn't know I could be that brutal. So I have hung back from life. Maybe I've been a little too kind, a little too patient in the name of love. Billy, please forgive me.

And since I'm asking for forgiveness, I'm sorry I frightened you Alice. I'm even more sorry I never talked to you again. I hope you understand. I was just a kid and it was pretty confusing. I tried to help you and ended up terrifying you.

As for you, God, I'm not sure if I can forgive you. What the hell were you thinking when you put the three of us on that playground? Where were you? Were you too busy writing commandments that day to get involved? Were you too busy running the world to stop three kids from having a wreck on the playground? What is wrong with you? Don't you care? I don't know. Yes, yes, I know. People say you talk, but we don't listen. You know what? That's bullshit, God. Really. I listen. I do my best with what I have. I think most people do.

Letters to My Friends

While we're talking, God, let me confess something. I would hit Billy again if he teased Alice. See, God, I wouldn't be able to stand by. I would like to think I wouldn't hit him as hard. And maybe I would only hit him one or two times. I'd like to think I would feel more compassion for him when I punched him. But I would punch him. I would punch you if you teased Alice. Somebody had to protect her. How else could I live with myself? So, you tell me God, did I do the right thing?

One more thing, God. Why is it that being loving and compassionate means making choices between what is right and what is right? It's confusing being here sometimes, isn't it? I do forgive you. If it's this hard for me, it has to be even harder for you. Take care, God.

Blessings,
    John Conley

John C. Conley

Questioner: Baba Ram Jahn, did you ever get in fights when you were a kid?

Baba Ram Jahn: No, my child, even then I had mystical powers which protected me.

Questioner: Oh, that is wonderful! Could you teach me these powers?

Baba Ram Jahn: No, daughter, I am sorry. My mystical powers are old now. But when I was a kid, all the other kids knew if they picked on me he would beat them up.

Questioner: "He?" Did you have a name for your mystical powers, Master?

Baba Ram Jahn: Yes, of course, mystical powers come in many forms. This form was my big brother. He was very big, very tough, and very powerful.

May 29

Dear Friends,

Who among us is blessed? There is only one true answer, or so I believe. Those of us who have touched Stillness are blessed. Stillness belongs to no one. Stillness cannot be understood or captured by a theology. Stillness is beyond us, yet within us. Stillness is the rush of a hurricane. Stillness is the smile of a baby. Stillness cries at our every woe. Stillness cannot be understood. Yet with every breath we imbibe it. We can dive in it, and though we swim forever, we will never reach its shores.

Stillness is here always. There is nothing we need to do or say. Nothing we need to understand. There are no mountains to climb. No scriptures to learn. No commandments to follow. There are no secret initiations, no chosen people, no rituals. Stillness simply is, and is as it is, always.

This Stillness is spoken of in the Vedas and the Bhagavad-Gita. It is spoken of in the Bible. It is spoken of in the Koran. It is spoken of in the holy scriptures of the Buddhists. Through many teachings it has survived. In one age it is called one thing, and in another age, it is called yet another thing. Today, here, now, I am calling it Stillness. But that, truly, is only a name and is not Stillness itself.

Yet, do not be misled. Stillness is not always quiet. Stillness is also the glint in the eye before a funny story is told. It is the excitement in the eyes of child at the top of a roller coaster. It is the smile of a lover and the feeling of awe in the heart of the beloved. It is our feeling of abundance when we walk through a poppy-laden meadow next to a clear, mountain stream. Stillness is the expression of our humanity as well as our divinity.

When I rest in Stillness, I am a lion roaring in the jungle. I am an eagle flying through a cloudless sky. I am a mighty river flowing to the sea. When I squat solely in my own mind, I am a hyena skulking in the desert. I am a crow screaming at the world. I am a puddle of dirty water.

When I rest in Stillness. I am at peace, wishing to harm no one. Yet, I take action, strong action. I stand up for what I think is right. I take my duties seriously and try my best to fulfill them. Nor am I afraid to refrain from action. Nor do I concern myself with results, for they do not rest in my domain, but with the larger domain of Stillness.

This is the secret of Stillness. As Krishna said to Arjuna, "You have a right to your actions, but not to the fruits of your actions." In Stillness, I take action. In Stillness, I step back from my action. If another action is needed, I take action. I step back. This passionate engagement and disengagement leads to a harmonious life. This, or so I believe, is the essence of all spiritual teachings.

To lead a full life, knowing that our lives are but small fragments of the whole, is that not our calling? To laugh hard, love deep, and grieve at a true loss, is this not our calling? To see the transitory nature of our laughter, our love, and our grief, is this not too our calling? This—to be human, to be divinely human—is the paradox and the beauty of our lives.

Therefore, live fully. Laugh when laughter is due. Love when love is due. Grieve when grief is due. But do all these things knowing they are autumn leaves floating on the vast river of consciousness that is Stillness. Do not let go of your humanity. Embrace it. And do not let go of Stillness. Embrace it.

Letters to My Friends

Live. Live fully. Kiss a boy. Hug a child. Hold a hand. Ride a bike. Laugh. Cry. Be outraged at injustice. By doing this and doing this fully, we can fully manifest Stillness. For Stillness, the ultimate creative force, the source of all things living and all things dead, the source of all time, past, present and future, this powerful Stillness does not want to be stale. Nor should you be.

So, now, close your eyes. Breathe in deeply and as you do imagine you are drawing energy into every fiber of your body. Imagine every fiber of your body is singing and dancing without restraint. Now, as you breathe out, send this energy into the world. What next? Do the same thing again and again and again. Soon, very soon, you will sense a deeper Stillness underlying this felt sense of energy. Go into that Stillness. Trust it. Do this a thousand times today, and today your life will be a thousand times better. Do it a thousand times tomorrow, and tomorrow your life will be a thousand times better. Do not tarry. Act now. But do not worry, for Stillness is as patient as it is vast. Stillness has all the time in the world. It will wait for you and for me.

Thank you,
    John Conley

Questioner: Baba Ram Jahn, would you please explain silence to me.

Baba Ram Jahn: Silence is what happens when you are asleep, questioner. I am married. I have children. I have a job. I am getting old. My hair is gone. So what I do is go into the noise. We find God in chaos and noise. As a matter of fact, I am thinking of starting a "Noise Meditation Group." In it everyone will talk at the same time. We will all bring our children and have them play in the circle, or if they are teenagers they can play loud music and roll their eyes while we talk to them.

Every week we will have guest managers from the business world, and they will tell us that our jobs are threatened and we are going to be downsized. We will have guest policemen, who will give us speeding tickets. We will have guest store clerks, who will be rude and unhelpful. And during all of this, my child, we will practice Stillness. We will follow the joy of life manifested in our bodies into Stillness. This will get us ready for the real world. We will go into the noise. If you want silence, get earplugs.

Questioner: Yes, yes, Baba, I see what you mean. We practice silence within, not without, because the world is not quiet. I see! We could stage medical emergencies on some weeks. We could invite ambulance drivers. We could

Baba Ram Jahn: Yes, yes, questioner. Please do not get carried away with this. And please be quiet. I need a little silence. As the wise ones say, "Silence is golden."

June 5

Dear Friends,

  Is a horse truer than a snake? Is a tree truer than a flower? Is the morning breeze truer than the evening breeze? Is the day truer than the night? Is the summer truer than the winter? Where does truth abide? I do not know, so I enter into Stillness and there I find peace.

  Are my beliefs more true than yours, or yours more true than mine? Is my experience more true than yours, or yours more true than mine? Am I more true than you, or you more true than I? Where does truth abide? Does it abide in our beliefs, our traditions, in those things we hold to be sacred? Does truth abide in rituals? Where does truth abide? I do not know, so I enter into Stillness, and there I find peace.

  Do I suffer? Do you suffer? Is my suffering real? Do I give it power when I say it is real? But if it is not real, then how could I give it power? Do I suffer because I have done something to deserve it? Did I do something wrong in this life? Did I do something wrong in a past life? Do I have past lives? Even if I did, and even if I remembered them, how could I possibly be sure I was not imagining them? Did my parents do something wrong? Did their parents do something wrong? Is a vengeful god punishing me for the sins of my ancestors? Where does truth abide? I do not know, so I enter into Stillness, and there I find peace.

  Do I have to work for my salvation, if there is such a thing? Or, if there is such a thing as enlightenment, do I have to work for it? Is my whole life fated, inevitable? Should I sit and wait for my awakening? The threads of my creation, do they extend backwards like spools of thread unwinding to eternity? Has my future already unspooled before me? Do I have any choice? Is there anything I can really do to better my life? "Stand up and fight, Arjuna," so implored Krishna of his friend and disciple in the Bhagavad-Gita. Should I stand up and fight? Should you? And Jesus said, "All ye who are heavy laden, come unto me and rest." Should I rest? Should I rest and then fight? My poor mind reels. Where does truth abide? I do not know, so I enter into Stillness and there I find peace.

Should I choose a religion in which to believe? There are times for all of us when we would like a guide through the thicket of our lives. Should I be a Hindu? Should I be a Muslim? Should I be a Jew? Should I be a Christian? Or perhaps I should be a Buddhist? I love the Bhagavad-Gita. It swells my heart with hope and courage. Reading about Mohammed fills my heart with devotion, for he was the most devoted of men. His love for God knew no end. The Jewish religion is ancient, and there is much to be loved in it. King David is a teacher for us all. And I still believe Jesus loves all the little children in the world; all of them—yours, theirs, and mine. And Buddha, his wisdom and compassion are surpassed by none. Where does truth abide? I do not know, so I enter into Stillness, and there I find peace.

Perhaps I should forget about religions and simply choose a practice. I could practice the Zazen meditation of Japan. I could practice the Tonglen meditation of Tibet. I have secretly always wanted to dance. Perhaps I could practice Sufi dances? I could chant a mantra, such as *Aum Mani Padme Hum*. Or I could recite the Lord's Prayer. Or more simply, I could repeat the name of Jesus. I could practice Jewish mysticism and live in the desert. Or I could take up Tai Chi or yoga. All of these things are good, of that I am sure. Yet I wonder. Where does truth abide? I do not know, so I enter into Stillness, and there I find peace.

I suppose I could choose a teacher and follow that teacher with complete dedication. Perhaps this is what I should do. I could follow somebody, anybody, who knows the secret of life and who will tell it to me. I could read a thousand more books and attend a hundred more seminars. I could discuss the spiritual life with everyone I meet. I could confuse myself so much that confusion becomes my best friend. I could take a stand. I could say this is what Jesus meant. And you are wrong, the only real meditation is sitting in Stillness, saying nothing. Yes, I could take a stand. I could even start my own religion, and why not? There is always room for another religion. I could gather together a little following, allow it to grow, and then spread the Truth according to John. Yes, I could take a stand. But I would be wrong. And I would always wonder. Where does truth abide? I do not know, so I enter into Stillness, and there I find peace.

Where does truth abide? It abides in my heart, in the Stillness of my heart. It is only in my heart that I find Stillness. And when I enter into that Stillness, it is the truth only for that moment. Truth for me is not a doctrine or a creed. And no one person contains the truth anymore than any other. Therefore, I am joyously wrong. I rest in the tranquility of not knowing. I embrace not knowing, for it is in not knowing, in relinquishing knowing, that I find my truth. I have no need to know. But I have a great need to be still. What then is truer? I do not know, so I enter into Stillness and there I find peace.

Thank you,
    John Conley

Questioner: Baba Ram Jahn, could you please talk about channeling? Specifically, could you explain how to do it?

Baba Ram Jahn: Questioner, sometimes you ask some of the strangest questions. Yet, there is a spiritual aspect to all situations. First, my daughter, you find the remote control and then sit in a comfortable chair. Then, questioner, you start to flick through the channels, watching each one briefly.

Questioner: But, Baba Ram Jahn, I think you misunderstood me. I was talking about ancient deities and . . .

Baba Ram Jahn: Patience, child, we have not yet come to the spiritual part. And just what is the spiritual part of channeling? There are many, to be sure. One in particular comes to mind. Suppose you find a channel you really like. It does not have to be a rerun, or an ancient deity, as you put it.

    First focus on that which you see. Then, focus on the act of seeing. Next focus on the mind as it interprets that which is seen. And finally, focus on the awareness behind the mind. It is almost as though you are breathing that which is seen through your eyes and sending it to Stillness. Yes, breathe through your eyes into Stillness.

    You look confused, my daughter. There is truth here for those who can see it. Wait. Wait, my child. What are you doing?

Questioner: I am doing exactly what you said, Master.

Baba Ram Jahn: Yes my daughter. But perhaps you should start with less advanced channeling first. I am not sure if "The World's Ten Greatest Hunks" was what I had in mind.

June 12

Dear Friends,

    Is there a difference between accepting a situation and resigning ourselves to it? I believe there is. If we accept a situation, we may speak out strongly against it. We may oppose it. But we do this from Stillness. Resigning ourselves to a situation means we quit. We acquiesce.

    Does accepting a negative situation mean we have to look for positive aspects in it? No, it does not. A horrible situation is a horrible situation. We do not need to hide a horrible situation with a layer of positive thinking. We need to hold that negative situation in Stillness, for again, that is true acceptance.

    Does the mere fact that we are happy mean that we are accepting? No, it does not. It only means we are happy. We are responding in a favorable way to something we like. We spend a week at the beach and we are happy. What does this have to do with acceptance? We need to take our happiness into Stillness. Conversely, if we are unhappy, does that mean we are not accepting? No, it does not. It only means we are unhappy. We are responding in a natural way to a negative situation. This is perfectly acceptable! We need to take our unhappiness into Stillness.

    If acceptance is not happiness, then what is it? If acceptance is not positive thinking, then what is it? Acceptance is not a thought. It is beyond thought. Acceptance is an attitude that arises from Stillness. We accept the moment, not the situation, not the story.

    I still have a strong sense of right and wrong. I know this is against much of the thinking of many teachers. We constantly hear, "It is all good." Or, "It is all God." Or, "There are no accidents." And that is true. Ultimately, everything is a unified field of consciousness. Our lives extend backward and forward in an intricate, multi-dimensional web for eternity.

But we do not live in the ultimate field of consciousness in our everyday life. We live here and now. We live in a world where corporations exploit the earth and dirty the water. We live in a world where religious fanatics attack and destroy those who do not believe as they do. We live in a world where children are abused, where women are still treated like slaves, where whole families die of hunger every day.

What are we to say of this? Are we to say that ultimately all things are one? Are we to say that suffering is an illusion? And what are we to do? Are we to sit in meditation and ignore the world? Are we to find our own enlightenment and ignore the world? I speak only for myself when I ask, "Is this acceptance?" And I speak only for myself when I say, "No this is delusion."

What did Jesus do? What did Buddha do? Did they stand aside and allow the rest of us to suffer? No, they served us with their lives. Did they say that in this world there is no suffering? No, they did not. Did they say that there is no right and wrong? No, they did not, not in this world at least. And they did everything they could to stop wrongdoing. And both of them said in their own way, "Do unto others as you would have them do unto you." They taught that there is a right way and wrong way to treat each other.

I say then if you see something wrong in your family, speak out. If you see something wrong in your work, speak out. If you see something wrong in your community, speak out. If you see something wrong in your nation, speak out. If you see something wrong in your world, speak out. Being voiceless is not acceptance. You will make some people angry, even if you speak gently and without anger. But others will welcome your voice.

If we abide in Stillness, we will not be consumed by the wrongs of this world, even while we speak out against them. If we abide in Stillness, we will know a true humility, and thereby allow ourselves to understand the views of those whose ideas we oppose. If we abide in Stillness, even if we speak out against an ill, we will do so from love and concern, not from hate and control.

True acceptance arises from Stillness. True acceptance is forceful, but never strident, never false, never arrogant, or conceited. True acceptance recognizes suffering and it recognizes that ultimately there is no suffering. True acceptance can change the world. Jesus showed us this. Buddha showed us this. Gandhi showed us this. Martin Luther King showed us this. And now perhaps it is our turn to show ourselves this. Perhaps it is time to accept our destiny.

Blessings,
    John Conley

Questioner: Baba Ram, could you explain the nature of life?

Baba Ram Jahn: Yes, I can. But you must understand that once one reaches enlightenment, all such questions become meaningless. In other words, questioner, I am that which you are not.

Once you have attained an enlightened state, you will be that which I am now, but by then I will not be that.

It is written in the sand which is ever changing with the tides of time that who you are is not who you are, and what you think is not what you think, and that which you feel is not what you feel.

And that, of course, is a good thing because some people are very strange and they are set free by being who they are.

Therefore, questioner, neither you nor I exist, except in the sand, which is timeless.

Now, any more questions? None? Good. Because I suddenly feel very hungry.

Summer

June 19

Dear Friends

Each moment we begin anew. Each moment our old self dies. And without this death, nothing new arises. We cannot cling to our old thoughts, habits, and patterns and expect to grow. We must die to them. This takes courage and discipline, both of which come about naturally from our practice of Stillness. We must practice always, day and night, without fail. We must practice dying and we must practice turning to our new selves. Christ saw this.

We must practice with the zeal and determination of a champion athlete. A champion practices every day. A champion does not quit. And when a champion grows discouraged, she keeps practicing, knowing that she cannot allow her moods to rule her life.

No champion would sit, never practicing, never striving to improve, and expect to win a competition. If she did, we would all be amazed. If we were cruel, we might laugh at her. If we were kind, we might offer her encouragement. But never, if we were honest, would we tell her that she would attain her goal by not practicing.

If we were a good friend, we would tell her to stand up and get to work. We would tell her not to give in to her fear. We might tell her to strive mightily, to do her best, and not be concerned if she wins or loses. We would tell her that while she can control her practice, she cannot control the results of her practice. This is the wisdom that has been passed down from generation to generation for thousands of years. It is ancient yet ever new.

And what is our competition, yours and mine? What do we strive to accomplish? Which race are we running? In a sense, we strive to accomplish our own death. We strive to die to our greed, our hatred, our rage, and fear. Our competition is life. Our practice is Stillness.

As we can only learn to run faster by running faster, we can only enter into Stillness by entering into Stillness. We must practice and we must practice diligently, for if we do not, the day will come when life will grab us by the throat, shake us, throw us down, and kick us. And if we have not entered into the Stillness so many times that the doorways into it are familiar, we will be lost. We will fall prey to our own fear, greed, resentment, and remorse. I know this to be true!

But I also know this to be true. If we enter into Stillness until it becomes our refuge, our home, then nothing can shake us from it. Yes, we might be buffeted like a great ship in a hurricane. Our sails may be shredded and our masts snapped as though they were twigs. But the ship of our Stillness will not flounder or sink.

Jesus said, "All ye who are heavily laden come unto me." In saying this, he called us into Stillness, into God. He meant that this Stillness, called by many names by many teachers, abides forever within us. All we must do is turn toward it. Step into it.

But, of course, the question is as it has always been, "How do we enter into Stillness?" Buddha had this to say, "One who conquers himself is greater than another who conquers a thousand times a thousand on the battlefield. Be victorious over yourself and not over others. When you attain victory over yourself, not even the gods can turn it into defeat."

To conquer themselves, I have been told, the Buddha taught his followers to meditate.

The purpose of meditation is to enter into Stillness. Each of us will find our own meditation, one that is uniquely suited to us. But here is what I do. Whether I am formally meditating for an afternoon, or whether I am talking to my children, working, or taking a walk, this is what I do. Perhaps it will work for you.

I breathe and I feel the energy flowing into my body. I feel it from my head to my toes. I breathe through my heart and my heart pulls in this energy. I breathe through my heart and my heart releases this energy as a blessing to the world, a small blessing given in love. I do not try to stop thinking. My thoughts float on the river of this energy and are absorbed into my heart and released as a blessing. I focus my attention on this energy and it leads me into Stillness. That is all I do. And the peace I feel is indescribable. Am I enlightened? God forbid, for then I might expect myself to do or say something profound, or to be perfect and without flaws. Have I found the ultimate truth? Again, God forbid. In an infinite universe how can there be an ultimate truth?

What I have found is peace of mind. On some days the flow of that peace is deep and wide, on other days it is a trickle. But the flow is there, always.

Thank you,
John Conley

Questioner: Could you please explain the nature of anger to me?

Baba Ram Jahn: No. Go away and leave me alone.

June 26

Dear Friends

If, to my children, I were to leave one path for them to follow, it would be this. Follow the path of Stillness. It has taken me years to realize this simple truth. And my finding it has not been easy, for I have been driven by anger and fear, by rage and hate. I have allowed resentments to consume me. I have hurt more people than I can remember. I do not even remember many of their names.

Yet, here I am, feeling a peace of such depth that I cannot describe it. I have done nothing to earn it. I have done nothing to deserve it. It is by a grace that passes my understanding that I have received it. Nor have I done anything that could prevent me from knowing it. No wrong could keep me from it. Eternity is forever, and I have had eternity to find it. Stillness is there always for all of us, rich and poor, good and bad. Nothing, not even our own fear, can keep us from the Stillness.

Yet, looking back through the years of pain and turmoil, I wish that I could have turned to Stillness somehow, someway, just a little sooner, with a little more strength; and in doing so, I could have saved both myself and others some measure of pain.

But my vision of this Stillness was blocked by pride and arrogance, by conceit and rebellion. I thought if I read one more book, I would understand the answer. If I attended one more lecture, I would understand the answer. Somehow, someway, I would find the answer, on my own. Most of all, however, my vision was blocked by my own desperation. I was in so much pain, I could not sit, just sit and sink into Stillness.

But somewhere along the way, I learned to sit with my pain. I learned to forgive myself. I learned to forgive others. I learned to make every waking moment a meditation, an entering into Stillness.

Life beat me down again and again before I learned this. And, may God help me, I am still learning it, in which case, I may be beaten down again. But this time I will know to sit with my pain, to take it into Stillness, to do this until the pain is transformed into joy. I know that I do not have to understand my pain to overcome it. I have learned to sit with my pain until my questions recede into unimportance. The questions never end. Why do I need to understand why I cause myself so much pain when I know how to end the pain? I do not need to know. I only need to be still.

So what is it I would tell my children? First, I would tell them nothing; rather I would ask them for a gift, the gift of forgiveness. I would ask them to forgive me for ignoring them. I would ask them to forgive me for every angry word. I would ask them to forgive me for my impatience and confusion. I would ask them to forgive me for not knowing how to be a better father.

And I would tell them that by forgiving me they would release themselves from any chains by which I bind them. In forgiving me, they would free themselves to fly, to glide into an inner freedom that only a few know. And then, after asking for forgiveness, I would tell them about Stillness and how to enter into it. I might ask them to remember a wonderful moment with me, a time when we felt good together, and I would tell them to follow that joy, that simple feeling of joy into Stillness.

And then this is what I would say to them. I would say, "Take that feeling of Stillness with you wherever you go. You are young, and when it is young, Stillness loves to run and play. It loves to jump in the water and it loves to get dirty. It loves being in love with a girl and it loves being in love with a boy. It loves being rowdy. It loves being loud and boisterous. This Stillness is a peacock. This Stillness is a giraffe and an elephant, and a centipede. How can you be any less flamboyant?"

And then I would say, "But remember also to sit with Stillness in quiet times of joy. Remember to sit with it when you feel rejected and confused. For this Stillness will heal you and guide you. This Stillness is beyond anything you or I have ever learned. Scriptures and holy books do not capture it. Priests speak of its shadow, not of its essence. It cannot be held captive like a bird in a cage. But it can be experienced like a bird soaring though a sunlit sky. So rejoice and be happy. Give your love to all you meet."

That, my friends, is what I would say to my children. And then I would say, "And remember me with fondness, not anger. Remember the love I have for you. If that Stillness starts to slip away, remember me with joy, and follow that joy to Stillness."

Be rowdy,
    John Conley

    Questioner: Master, what can one say about Stillness?

    Baba Ram Jahn: Many, many books have been written about Stillness, my daughter. I have read books about how to find Stillness and how to be and live in Stillness. But really, only one thing can be said about Stillness.

    Questioner: And what is that, Master?

    Baba Ram Jahn:

    Questioner: Master, Master, did you hear me?

July 3

Dear Friends,

What is freedom? I know only what it is for me. When my mind is quiet, I am free. It is simple. Freedom is a quiet mind and a quiet mind is freedom. This freedom is beyond the understanding of my mind. But that is not a bad thing, for freedom is an experience of the infinite, not an understanding of the infinite.

Nor do I believe it is, as many of us have been taught, freedom from lack. If by freedom, we mean that we will always have reliable cars, satisfying romances, and comfortable houses, we will be disappointed, for outward things always change. If by freedom we mean that we will always love our work and find it satisfying, we will be disappointed, for outward things always change. If by freedom, we mean that we will never be sick, then we will be disappointed, for outward things always change. On the other hand, it is not that these outward things are not enjoyable, for they are. But what is outside of us will not set us free.

But if freedom is an experience of the infinite, does that then mean we will move beyond all desire and eventually live in a state of utter bliss, never disturbed by the passing march of humanity? No, or at least that has not been my experience, nor have I met anyone who has had that experience. This does not mean that these blissful beings do not exist, but they are few, and my path is not theirs, nor do I want it to be. The freedom I seek is the freedom to live more fully as a man, to love and laugh more fully, to feel sorrow and weep more fully. My destiny is not to transcend this life, but to be fulfilled in it. Bliss is not a bad thing, but it will not set us free.

Letters to My Friends

No, that has not been my experience at all, the state of eternal bliss. Three months ago I yelled at my daughter for no better reason than I was tired, and I felt ashamed. Two weeks ago I yelled at my wife, for no better reason than I was worried, and I felt ashamed. Last week, I threatened to eat one of our numerous cats when she vomited on the rug after being outside all day.

I get afraid of losing my job. I worry about money. When I get a new wrinkle, I think how unfair life is. I want to run away and hide. I want everyone to leave me alone. I want to sit in the forest and meditate all day long and leave all strife and turmoil behind. Yet, I tell you with all sincerity, I have found freedom. I have a quiet mind and a peaceful heart.

How can this be? Am I deluded? Some would say so. Am I lost in grandiose fantasies? Personally, I think those are the best kind, but I do not feel lost. No, I feel free. I feel free of the need to be right. I feel free of the need to control others. I feel free of the need to control situations.

In short, I am a spiritual human being. I am the waves on the surface of the sea, but I am also the deep waters underneath. I am the autumn breeze, flitting here and there, but I am also the northern mountains from which the breeze is born. I am the leaf of the giant oak, but also the root. I believe this to be true because when my mind is quiet, I sense this infinite greatness. Even when my mind is busy directing the universe and all the creatures in it, I am aware of the Stillness underneath. To me that is freedom.

Knowing this Stillness, not being perfect or having a perfect life, is freedom. Perhaps some day, I will sit in front of a cave and blissfully meditate day and night, while my devotees bring me fruit and flowers, but until that day, I am free.

John C. Conley

So, of course, the question is as it always is, "How do we find this quietness of mind, this freedom, this Stillness?" And the answer is as it always is, "We focus on that underlying Stillness, the mountain from which springs the breeze. We focus on the root of the tree." We focus on Stillness so much that we realize it is as much a part of us as our chattering minds. Then we focus on it until the chattering grows quieter and we become the Stillness.

We expect nothing. We simply focus on this Stillness. If we get angry, we apologize, make amends, and focus on this Stillness. If we have questions about the meaning of life, ones that we feel must be answered for us to be happy, we laugh at ourselves, and focus on this Stillness. If we get sick, we focus on this Stillness. If we lose our jobs, we focus on this Stillness. If our country elects the wrong man as president, we focus on this Stillness. If our country goes to war, we focus on this Stillness. That is all we do, and this will revolutionize our lives and set us free from ourselves. This is freedom. This is Stillness.

So now, close your eyes. Breathe in this Stillness through your heart. Breathe out this Stillness through your heart. Feel it in every fiber of your being. Keep doing this. Laugh at yourself. Do not take yourself too seriously. Simply breathe this Stillness with your heart. That is really all you need to do. But if rituals, steps, and traditions help you to do this, then by all means follow the rituals, steps, and traditions. But do not forget the Stillness. Never forget the Stillness.

Thank you,
John Conley

Letters to My Friends

Questioner: Baba Ram Jahn, tell me about mistakes.

Baba Ram Jahn: If I had cried every time I made a mistake, I would have drowned by now in the pool of my tears. Therefore, my daughter, I say this. When tears come, welcome them as a gift, but do not swim in them.

July 10

Dear Friends,

    I interpret God in my intellect. I feel God in my heart. But this is not enough. There is a danger in that; for I cannot see God beyond my experience of myself. And I cannot see myself beyond my experience of my culture and my place in it. Simply put, this is why, to some, God is a God of love; and to others, God is a God of judgment.

    My experience is that a vastly greater number of people believe God is a king, one who rewards good and punishes evil. And of those who believe in God the king, the vast majority believe themselves to be His earthly army. And that is where we start to get into horrible trouble. It does not take a giant leap of imagination to see the Islamic world and the Christian world pitting themselves against each other and starting a war that will be bloodier than any that has come before it. The Jews will, of course, side with the Christians. The Hindus in India will side with the Christians. The Buddhist nations may try to remain neutral, but they will be drawn into this war too on the side of the Christians.

    And what will the result be? Blood, death, and destruction on a scale I can scarcely imagine, nor do I want to imagine it. I hope I am wrong. God, how I hope I am wrong. But I only have to listen to the rhetoric on both sides to become very, very frightened. This march toward total war has a feeling of inevitability about it. It would be very easy to acquiesce to my fears, to give up hope that we can live in a world of peace.

    But I will not acquiesce. My experience of fear is very much like my experience of Stillness. When I am rooted in Stillness, when I feel that profound sense of inner peace, everything around me feels peaceful. Strangers smile at me on the street. Clerks smile and ask about my day with genuine interest. Little kids run up to me and ask me to tie their shoes. But when I practice fear, how the world does change. Strangers avert their eyes. Clerks never smile. And children peek around their mother's legs.

It is not my intent to delve into who is right and who is wrong here in my country, the republicans or the democrats. Recently, fear seems to be infecting all Americans. I will say this, though. I am glad to be an American. With all our many faults—from the slaughter of American Indians to the enslavement of African Americans—I am still glad to be an American. It is not always our actions I love, rather it is our ideals. I suspect many of my friends could say the same of me. I am grateful to be able to write this letter without fear of reprisal from my government. I am grateful to be able to be a member of my local Unity Church. I have that choice, and it is one I value greatly.

So, my question to myself is this? What am I to do? As an American who loves my country, what am I to do? As a man, who loves peace, what am I do? As a man who loves God, who loves Stillness, what am I to do? What am I to do to avert the approaching insanity?

First, I will do everything in my power to experience a God who is beyond my intellect, who is beyond my emotions, and who is beyond my culture; because it is there, beyond my conceptions of God, that I will touch the ultimate mystery of the universe. This God is beyond words. This God can only be experienced.

But how do I know I am experiencing God? How do I know if my path is leading me to the mountain top and not to the swamps below? That is easy. I ask a few questions. Am I happy? Do I make other people happy? Am I glad to see myself in the morning? Are others glad to see me? Please say yes! Do I feel at peace with myself? Is that sense of peace growing?

After I make conscious contact with God as I understand Her, what else can I do to avert the insanity? I can tell anyone who will listen about my experience of the divine. For me it is clear that God does not prefer Jews over Christians; or Christians over Muslims; or Muslims over Hindus; or Hindus over Buddhists. God does not care about my interpretations of the divine. God cares only that I love. And I can only love when I am still.

So how do I express that love? How can I deploy that love to head off the forces of insanity? For me, for now, I love by not being caught up in the fear; which in turn allows me to send love in my prayers and meditations to those whom I fear. I send love to the presidents, prime ministers, and kings. I send love to imams, priests, rabbis, and preachers. I send love to the fighting soldiers and I send love to those whom they fight. I send love to all suffering people everywhere. And above all, I send love to those who love but feel frightened and powerless. From a place of Stillness, I simply surround the whole world in love.

Does anyone sense my love? Does it change their lives? Does it stir love in them? My heart tells me yes! Oh yes, yes, yes. Why else would strangers smile and clerks laugh? Why else would a little boy say, "Will you tie my shoe?" Why else?

Blessings,
    John Conley

Questioner: Master, tell me, do you think it is essential to sit in the lotus position while meditating?

Baba Ram Jahn: Much has been written about the proper position to assume while meditating. There are those who say it is best to stand on your head. And others who say that it is best to jump on one foot and chant, "I am a salamander." Then, of course, there is the adepts pose. And the nose pose. And the military pose. Of course, there is the famous pig pose, where one grunts and snuffles. None of these poses are especially worthy, except for the "I am a salamander" pose, naturally. But my favorite pose of them all is the slumping Om pose.

Questioner: I do not think I have heard of this pose, Baba. Could you explain it to me?

Baba Ram Jahn: Rather, my child let me demonstrate it for you.

Questioner: (several minutes later) But, Baba, you have not moved. You're still slumping in that old, overstuffed chair. You appear to be asleep!

Baba Ram Jahn: Huh? What? Oh yes. Precisely, my child. The slumping Om pose! Om. Om. Om . . .

Questioner: Baba, Baba! This is wonderful. You're snoring! Now where can I find that Zen stick?

July 17

Dear Friends,

I must go beyond concepts, not out of any lofty ideals of awakening, but rather for my own survival. Let me explain. We have all heard that God is love. This is in the Bible. God is love. But if that is so, then why are children born deformed? Why do mothers in India peck through cow manure to find food for their children? Why did the Nazis butcher twenty million Jews in World War II? Why did European settlers, who wanted nothing more than a better life, slaughter millions upon millions of Native Americans? Why do my friends suffer? Why do we grow old and sick and die, often alone and full of fear? Where is the love in that? Tell me, where is the love?

When I enter into Stillness, I enter into love and I leave these questions behind. I know that not one tear is shed by one child unless that which I call God also sheds a tear.

But, of course, God is love. It is human beings who are unloving. It is our karma. Have we not all heard that we chose this life after finishing our last life? We chose this life to work through our karma. Yes, of course, millions upon millions of Native Americans chose to be slaughtered. And ask any Jew, surely they will all agree that they chose to be butchered as a part of their collective karma. And, yes, that means millions of Germans chose to wield the butcher's knife. And the woman in India, pecking through the manure, she too chose her life. She chose to suffer. But tell me, where is the love in that? Where, please tell me, is the love in that?

You see? I must enter into Stillness, otherwise my mind leads me down these torturous paths where the answers to the questions outrage me and fill me with ridicule. I watched my mother die a slow agonizing death from cancer. From the time I was ten until I was nineteen, I watched her fight cancer. I never knew my mother. I knew a woman wracked by pain and riddled by drugs. Do you mean to tell me that she chose her life? Do you mean to tell me that I chose my life, that I numbed myself to her suffering simply so I could survive? I chose that?

But, when I enter into Stillness, I enter into love and I leave these questions behind. I know that not one tear is shed by one child unless that which I call God also sheds a tear. I know that God shed many tears for my mother and for me and for my father, brother, and sister. As we suffered, so did God.

We have also been told that life is a dance, an illusion. It's not real. It's not real when big business gives management a bonus for firing hundreds of employees to enhance the god of the bottom line. It's not real when developers dig up whole farms and plant huge houses that sprout up like ugly weeds and choke the landscape. It's a dance when the strong prey on the weak. It's a dance when one ghetto kid murders another. It's a dance when your mother commits suicide. It's a dance when your friend gets raped. It's all a dance. It's not real. That crying child over there in Iraq who just lost her mother to a suicide bomber is not real. She is dancing. But I am not dancing. I feel like vomiting when I hear that it is a dance. The only dance we do is the dance of running from our suffering, from explaining it into nonexistence.

But, when I enter into Stillness, I enter into love and I leave these questions behind. I know that not one tear is shed by one child unless that which I call God also sheds a tear. I know that somehow God is dancing and I want to dance also.

Many of us have learned that we are being punished for our sins by a loving and just God. We were born into sin and therefore we suffer. Now I see. I was born rotten. I will live rotten. And I will die rotten. I must ask for forgiveness and fear God. I must do good now to avoid hell and damnation for the rest of eternity. Now I understand suffering. God loves me, and therefore He will punish me forever and ever unless I do as He wants. Yes, God is punishing the crippled child. God is certainly punishing the old man in the nursing home who no longer recognizes his own wife. God is punishing the young soldier who just lost both legs in defense of his country.

Do you see? I must enter into Stillness. My mind simply cannot sustain a happy view of life. I ask too many questions. And the answers never satisfy me. I agree with no one, not Krishna, not Buddha, or Lao-tse, or Jesus, or Mohammed, or Billy Graham, or the Dalai Lama.

I am alone and it is only in Stillness that I find peace. It is only in Stillness that I find love. It is only in Stillness that I find joy. There, in Stillness, all my questions, all my doubts and fears, are answered with a resounding silence. Stillness takes me up into it, and I am comforted. I know that as I cry, as you cry, so does God cry. But I also know that as I laugh, as you laugh, God laughs. There is no answer but Stillness.

So, now, this minute, go there. Go to that still place and rest. If you can not find it, stop trying. Just sit and quiet your mind. The Stillness will arise without your help. If you cannot quiet your mind, then focus on the energy in your chest. As you breathe in, as you breathe out, feel the energy in your chest. Let this energy permeate every fiber of your being, for this is Stillness manifesting in your body. Live more in your body, and less in your mind.

And know this. Not one tear is shed by one child unless God also sheds a tear. And as God cries, so do we.

Thank you,
    John Conley

Letters to My Friends

Questioner: Master, what is the answer?

Baba Ram Jahn: My daughter, my dear daughter, the answer is compassion.

Questioner: But, Master, many times you have told me Stillness is the answer.

Baba Ram Jahn: Yes, this is true, child, but never have I said consistency is the answer!

July 24

Dear Friends,

    Let us speak of that which cannot be understood with words. There abides within each of us a force so ancient that even the oldest stone cannot tell us of its origins, for it has no origin. Yet, it is ever new. Not even a newborn babe, greeting the world with a bellow, can match its freshness. It is gentle, so very gentle. Not even the brush of a mother's lips on the cheeks of her little girl is more gentle. Yet it is fierce. Not even the stern lecture of an even sterner father is more fierce. But the fierceness is born of gentleness, not of judgment.

    I call this force Stillness. I know little about it. I know when I calm my mind, I feel loved. I know when I walk in Stillness, my step feels firm. I know when I look at my daughter, the depth of my love has no end, when I hold her in Stillness. I know I am fearless when I am in Stillness. I know that when I am still, I am in Stillness.

    I do not know if Mohammed was the last messenger of God. I do not know if Jesus rose from the dead. I do not know if Buddha showed us the ultimate truth. I do not know if Krishna stood with Arjuna in the chariot. But I do know that when I abide in Stillness, I feel a deep peace, one as deep as the deepest ocean, one as deep as the sky and the darkness beyond it.

    I do not know how to manifest wealth. Yet I am the wealthiest of men. I do not know how to defeat others and gain a promotion. Yet I feel promoted beyond all others. I say silly things to my wife and hurtful things to my children. Yet I am the wisest of men. In me all things that have ever been born exist. In me, all things that have not been, exist. For I am that Stillness and that Stillness is me.

Yes, I am the wisest of men, as wise as Solomon. I work. I meditate. I walk with my daughters, and now that I am older they wait for me. I argue with my son, for he is stubborn, much like me. I hold my wife's hand. I pet the cats and threaten to eat them when they annoy me. I do yoga, without grace but with much gratitude. I read holy books and understand little of what I read. I get worried. I get afraid.

I see a pretty girl and the teenage boy who lives still in me says, "Holy mackerel!" I watch sad movies with my wife and cry, and then I feel slightly ashamed. When I hear *The Star Spangled Banner*, I feel a lump in my throat and I put my hand on my heart. I love what this country can still be. I read *Harry Potter*.

But most of all, I am still. That is what I do. I read what the Buddha said I should do and I get confused. So I am still. I read what Mohammed said I should do, and I get confused, so I am still. Jesus, Moses, Krishna, they all speak to me through Holy Scriptures, and I get confused. But that is fine, for I am still.

Perhaps it is because I am so ignorant, but I think that too much knowledge keeps us from Stillness. If someone asked me what I thought, I would say, "Love knowledge, but do not think you need knowledge to enter into Stillness."

Nor do you need to be perfect, or even good, to enter Stillness. But a little compassion toward yourself and others will take you far. Greet your shortcomings with a smile and let them continue on their way. For what are shortcomings but thoughts about thoughts? Remember, you are Stillness.

I do not mean to say, however, that you should not honor your mind. It can be your willing ally on the path of Stillness. Your own mind will remind you to practice Stillness. Your own mind will tell you that Stillness, not knowledge, is your answer, your redemption. So be nice to your mind today.

And now what? Be still. Be still when you laugh. Be still when you wash the dishes. Be still when you change the diaper. And be still when you yell at your husband. Be still when you tell your wife, "I don't want to talk about it." Yes, be still, and remember, this Stillness is not hiding from you. It's not evasive or secretive. You do not have to climb a mountain, spiritual or otherwise. It's there, right inside of you. Just close your eyes and rummage around in your heart until you find a quiet spot. Then stay there.

Blessings,
    John Conley

Questioner: Master, if Stillness can not be understood with our minds, why do we speak of it? Why do we write about it and think about it?

Baba Ram Jahn: Child, we speak of it so that we can make believe we are doing something useful while we wait for Stillness to move through us.

Questioner: And I think, Master, it would be more useful to learn to surf or play the ukulele while we wait for Stillness. Surfing is very spiritual. And think of koans we could write. What is the sound of one foot surfing? If a surfer falls and no one sees it, did it really happen?

Baba Ram Jahn: We live in Oregon. The water here is cold!

Questioner: Yes, Baba, you are right. It is obvious. Stillness is calling us to Maui! I have attained Nirvana. I see the future!

July 31

Dear Friends,

This is my life. I have gone to a high mountain and found a cliff. I did this the day I was born. The drop from the cliff seems to go on forever. But it does not. It ends in my death. I jumped from that cliff the first day of my life and I have been falling ever since to my death. I cannot see the ground below me, but it is there, sweeping ever closer to me. And when I hit it, I will die. My death could come in any moment. But come it will and there is nothing, absolutely nothing I can do to stop it. And there are days when I am afraid.

How then should I face my fear, for face it I must.

Perhaps as I fall I should buy as many things as possible. I should buy a big house and a fancy car. I should go to the Bahamas every year. Perhaps I should spend nearly every waking hour of my life earning the money to do these things. There is nothing wrong with this life. Actually there is much good in it. The goods I buy will employ many people, and that is a good thing. And there is much bad in it. The goods I buy will one day deplete the earth of its blood. But, good or bad, living this life will not stop me from hitting the ground one day. It will not help me face my fear.

Or I could be a political activist. I could adopt a cause. I could save the whales. Or I could fight for the rights of indigenous people to kill the whales. I could save the trees or I could fight for the rights of mill workers. I could go to every rally and demonstration ever held. Again, there is nothing wrong with such a life. Much good can come from it. And, of course, much that is bad can come from it. But, good or bad, none of this will stop me from hitting the ground. None of it will stop my fear.

I am going to die. That is my inevitable end. I can fight it. I can ignore it. I can run and hide from it. I can practice positive thinking. I can believe in heaven. Or I can believe in karma. But I am going to die. I would like to die with dignity and grace. I do not want to cling to life like a little boy clinging to his mother's leg, peeking out from behind her at a frightening world. But that is sometimes how I feel. I feel afraid.

I would like to greet my death with a smile, with a wave of the hand, like a hero. I want to greet my death unencumbered by fear. And to do this, to greet death fearlessly, I must rid myself of all the beliefs that stand between me and death, that protect me from the knowledge of my own end.

Do I believe in heaven? Yes, I do, but this is a belief I must shed, for if I believe in heaven, then I must believe in earning my way into it, either through my own efforts, or through the interdiction of an outside force—God. Perhaps, to enter into heaven, I will need to believe in good people and bad people, and I will have to decide which is which. Perhaps I will need to love God, and perhaps I will be afraid when I do not. This belief in heaven is an encumbrance I do not need.

I also believe in karma, in good and evil, in positive thinking and negative thinking, and in the healing power of God. I believe America is a great country on the verge of mediocrity. I believe Canadians say "Eh" in every sentence so they will not be mistaken for Americans. I want God to bless our troops. And I want us all to love each other. I believe in love.

And, I believe that none of these beliefs will postpone my death by even one second. And not one of these beliefs, not even my most dearly held ones about God and the meaning of life will take me even one step from my fear.

Letters to My Friends

So, how then, am I suppose to live as I fall from the cliff to my death? In Stillness, of course. For in Stillness there are no questions and there are no answers. And, perhaps because of this, in Stillness there is no fear. There is no fear of being right, and no fear of being wrong.

So be still. Enter into Stillness daily. Know, at least in my world, that if you feel the urge to understand something, that this is not Stillness. It is your little self falling to its death. But always be compassionate to your little self. Love your little self. Take it to Maui if you can. Drive a Mustang convertible if you can. Take walks on the beach. Love your children. Take a deep breath and live fully. Give your little self the happiest life you can. Do not be a coward and hide.

But know that the Stillness is your larger Self. And in this larger Self, all the questions that seem so important become much less so. In Stillness, it is not that we will die or not die, fear or not fear, it is rather that death is not something we grant significance. In Stillness, I am not afraid of my own death, for the Stillness cradles my death and my fear of it ceases to matter.

So, be still. Be still when you laugh. Be still when you dance. Be still when you are afraid. Be still when you yell. Above all, as you fall from the cliff, be still and you will find the courage to live fully moment by moment. Be both human and divine. In the end, are they not the same? So, will my life end? Will I be dead forever and forever? Or will I live on forever and forever? I do not know. I only know that Stillness is much bigger than death, and when I am still, I am alive.

Blessings,
    John Conley

Questioner: Baba Ram Jahn! What are you doing? You're yelling and screaming and jumping up and down. Oh, I see, you are showing me that Stillness is an inner state, not an outer circumstance. You are so wise.

Baba Ram Jahn: Yes, my daughter, that is what I am trying to teach you. But I am not wise. It is the bee I stepped on who is wise!

August 7

Dear Friends,

Hug your children. Hold your wife in your arms and tell her you love her. Take a walk with your dog. Tell your husband he is your hero. Men want to be heroes. Find meaning in your work, and be a blessing to those with whom you work. Live life simply and well. That is the meaning of life I find in Stillness. I do not believe we are here in this life to overcome ourselves. We are not here to stamp out the evil that resides within in us. We are not here to overcome our egos. We are not here to go beyond ourselves. Who we are, what we are, in our everyday lives is holy. If there is a secret to life, I believe this it. We are holy in all our humanness.

We are meant to laugh and sing and dance. We are meant to walk on the beach, to spend time with friends, to throw sticks for dogs, and to pet purring cats. We are meant to work, meant to build a better place for our children. We are meant to succeed, not in collecting more money than we need, but to succeed in having enough. And we are meant to succeed in courage and love. We are all meant to be heroes, teachers, saints. We are meant to uplift those around us through our Stillness.

We are meant to be happy. No, again, I do not want to overcome myself. I do not want to leave myself behind to attain enlightenment. I want, rather, to align myself—my personality, this entity I call John—with Stillness.

Do I want to love more? Then I should enter Stillness. Do I want more friends? Then I should enter Stillness. Do I want more security? Then I should enter Stillness. Do I want someone to love me? Then I should enter Stillness. Am I confused and lonely? Then I should enter Stillness, for it is in Stillness that I will find the fulfillment of myself. In Stillness I will find courage, strength, and love. In Stillness I will be a magnificent me, not a frightened, lost me.

How do I know this? I know this because that has been my experience. Therefore, I know it only for myself. But I believe with all my heart that it is true for you also. You do not need to go through your life feeling afraid. I know little of karma, reincarnation, original sin, eternal hell, or eternal heaven. But I do know this. No matter what is true, it stems from Stillness, and this Stillness resides in me always.

If karma is true, then it is in Stillness that I will find good karma. If reincarnation is true, then it is in Stillness that I will find a better life in my next life. If original sin, heaven, and hell are true, then it is in Stillness that I will avoid sin and find heaven. At times it frightens me, but I do not want to be guided by commandments, lists, strictures, Holy Scriptures, or anything else outside of myself. Stillness is enough. This Stillness is as much a part of me as my hand. It is as supernatural and yet as ordinary as a sunset over the sea, one where the orange fire of the sun illuminates the whole horizon as it sets.

And if I stray from Stillness—and I will—and I do not know how to act, I can always ask myself if I am being nice. It is such a simple question, but it can keep us from being led astray when the inner path to Stillness is blocked by brambles of fear. Being nice can lead us back to Stillness.

Are you being nice? I do not care what you believe. I do not care if you are a Republican or a Democrat, liberal or conservative, a Mormon or a Muslim. I only care if you are nice. I do not care if you have been born again or if you are enlightened, and I do not care if you want to save me. I only care if you are being nice; for if you are nice, you are also still.

So, this is what I would say to you. Find a way to be still. Find a way to go underneath the chatter in your mind to something deeper. There is no need to destroy the chatter. Simply go underneath it. Go underneath it to that deep place, and live your life from there as much as you can. If you fail, and you will, go back to that deep place. If you become angry and fearful, or even full of rage and hate, go back to the deep place that is within you. Start again. Do you have a question? Take it to that deep place. Do you want to know if you should change jobs? Do you want to know if you should get married? Should you return to school? Should you bake potatoes or boil pasta for dinner?

Take all of this into Stillness. None of it is too mundane, too silly, too commonplace. This Stillness is mundane and commonplace too. It is only our absence from it that has caused us to think otherwise. Are you angry with your husband? Is your daughter driving you insane? Does the gas station attendant move too slowly? Is your last boyfriend a moron? Is your son taking drugs? Take them with you into your inner Stillness. Hold them there in your mind's eye, surrounded by love and light. Send them love and light. See them sending you love and light. You will be amazed at what happens. Your life will get better. This ordinary, mundane life will get better, for that is the way it is meant to be.

Blessings,
    John Conley

John C. Conley

Baba Ram Jahn: Questioner, I heard a wonderful joke. What do you call a drummer after his girlfriend kicks him out of the house? Homeless! And here is another one. Why did the drummer cross the road after the chicken? Because he was marching to a different drummer!

Questioner: As are you, Master. So, Master, I have a joke too. What does a drummer say between gigs? Pizza delivery boy!

Baba Ram Jahn: My daughter, I am shocked. Don't you think your joke shows a certain insensitivity to pizza delivery boys?

August 14

Dear Friends,

If positive thinking were the answer to the question of my life, would I not by now be living a perfect life? I have had many positive thoughts in my life, several today alone. And my life is nevertheless full of problems. My problems are real to me, and they require real solutions. One of my daughters is mad at me, and I have no idea why. I am worried about Islamic fundamentalists attempting to dominate the world. My work is increasingly dissatisfying. I am getting older, and I am not as full of energy as I once was. And money, of course, there never seems to be enough of that. My problems range from the worrisome to the seemingly overwhelming.

And no matter how hard I try to think positive thoughts, negative thoughts keep creeping into my mind and setting up camp like an invading army. There are times, when for no apparent reason, I become depressed and frightened. I dread what will happen next. Or, there are times when, again for no apparent reason, I loathe myself. Or, worse, there are times when I feel angry and hateful toward those I love.

Why is this? Why does this heathen army rage in my soul? The answer, my friends, seems simple, almost too simple. My soul, your souls, our souls rage because it is the way we are. From the minute we are born, we are destined to be angry, frightened, greedy, desperate, and hateful. This is the instinctive side of our ego. Read the sayings of Buddha in the Dhammapada. Read the Bhagavad-Gita. Read the Gospel according to Luke. We are born with the urge to destroy ourselves and those we love.

But here is the good news. We are born also with the urge and the capacity to transcend ourselves, to transform ourselves, to align ourselves with something much more powerful than our lower selves. For most of us, transforming ourselves requires work, work, and more work. Slow learning is deep learning. This transformation requires much time spent in meditation, much time spent in prayer, and much time spent in service. Each of us will be drawn to one of these paths more so than the others, but balance is a good thing.

By meditation, I mean touching that inner Stillness that resides in all of us. Some call it Consciousness. Some call it Buddha nature. I call it Stillness because that is my experience of it. By prayer I mean holding those for whom we are praying in the light of this Stillness. When I pray, I visualize, for example, my son surrounded by a loving light. I see him absorbing this light and spreading it to others. Pray for those you love, and for those you do not love. That is my simple definition of prayer. By service, I mean helping others. For me, this usually means helping my own family and sometimes my community. It also means sponsoring a meditation group. For me, in other words, service presents itself in my everyday life. We do not have to leave our homes and dedicate ourselves to feeding the hungry to serve others.

My belief is that I will always be prone to the attacks of my lower nature, no matter how far along the spiritual path I am. And let me make it clear what I mean by my lower nature. This is the side of me that is literally destructive of life. We all have that side. It is from that we are escaping. This is the side that gets fearful, angry, resentful, hateful, greedy. This is the side that many teachers call the ego, and when they speak of it, they speak of it as the enemy. This lower nature of ours can be violent both towards ourselves and others. We all, God help us, have a predator in us.

But it is not the enemy. It is not something to hate and despise. Again, this lower nature, this urge toward destruction, is simply a part of us. It is as though we are living with a ravenous monster, and that monster is us. As long as we are aware of the monster, it can do us little harm. But if we ever think we no longer have a monster dwelling within us, then we are in trouble. Then the monster has fooled us.

To put it another way, there are parts of our personality that will align with our spiritual growth. Our love of beauty, our desire to be held and comforted, our desire to grow and explore, even our desire to make love will align with our higher natures. But each of us also has this predatory side, and I do not think this part of us ever completely dies. We each have a destructive facet to the diamond that is ourselves. But we do not have to live in fear of that facet. Knowing it is there is enough. By recognizing it, by seeing it for what it is, we will not cut ourselves on its jagged edge. Do not be afraid, but be careful.

So where does this leave us? It leaves us with Stillness and the practice of Stillness. It leaves us with prayer and service. Do these things and your thoughts will become positive, not because of your effort to make them so, but because they will arise as a result of your actions which in turn come from Stillness.

So, be still and know that God is God. And know that whether you are on the first step of your spiritual journey or the thousandth step, it matters not one iota to God. All that matters is the journey and the step before you now.

Blessings,
    John Conley

John C. Conley

Questioner: Baba Ram Jahn, is it true that a beaver is wiser and more powerful than a duck? Is it true that in the game of life that beavers trounce on ducks? Is it true that ducks fly back and forth on the field of life, going nowhere, doing nothing, never reaching their goal?

Baba Ram Jahn: My dear daughter, God loves all animals equally. Who am I to denounce furry little creatures with flat tails and little pointed heads? True, beavers are ugly and not too bright, and they smell bad too. But God loves them. Look, daughter, I see one now. What is it doing? It's wandering aimlessly on the field of life!

August 21

Dear Friends,

Please do not judge me for my little jealousies. Do not judge me for my harsh words. Do not judge me for my fear and despair. No, judge me, please, on my willingness to love. For it is love that makes me who I am. It is love that sets me apart from my judgment of myself. And it is love that saves me.

If I fail a thousand times a day, but am willing to love, then that is all that matters. My failures are nothing compared to my love. And, in truth, there are no failures, for in the end, all things reach for God, even those that seem the most vile and disgusting to my human eyes.

It is love that makes me who I am. It is love that prompts me to enter daily into Stillness; love for my world, love for my country, love for my state, love for my family, and love for myself. If I had not love, would I seek Stillness? I would not.

Stillness is the edge of God and Stillness nurtures the love within me. It is in Stillness that I learn to meld Divine love with the love in my heart. When I am still, I feel compassion toward myself. And I know in this compassion is where the love of God meets my love. I meld with God and we are both enriched. The love of the cosmos is not complete until it meets the love of the heart. And it is in that new love that God learns to cry.

I know I have not explained this well. Here is a story. There was once a Buddhist monk, a master really, named Chin, who lived in a mountainous region in a small country near China one thousand years ago. Master Chin sat in the bamboo forests and meditated day after day, year after year until he saw the world for what it was, impersonal and transient. His calmness grew to such immense proportions that panda bears would sit by him calmly. The vicious thieves of the mountains were so in awe of him that they left him gifts of food.

But there was one thief who was the biggest thief of all, and her name was Ling Su. She stole that which was most precious. One day the chief of the thieves approached Chin, and said, "Master, our work, as you know, takes us far and wide." The chief had the grace to look a little sheepish. "Be that as it may, we worry about you. Especially in the winter, who will bring you food when we are gone?"

Master Chin nodded and smiled, but said nothing. In truth, he was barely aware of the chief. The chief continued, "I will leave this orphan, Ling Su, here with you this winter with enough food for the both of you. Her mother and father died in a raid upon our village. She will bring you food, and no one will dare to harm her if she is in your protection."

Master Chin nodded and smiled. And so it came to pass that for many years, Ling Su brought the master rice and vegetables everyday from the village of the thieves, where she lived with her aunt, who was married to the chief. Once on her tenth birthday, after she had been coming for three years, she felt bold, and after she gave the master his food, she sat by him. And from that day on she sat by him. Soon she even looked like a minor Master Chin. She sat in the lotus position and gazed placidly at the world through brown eyes, free of greed.

As the years passed, the panda bears sat by her side. The tigers curled at her feet. Calm radiated from her like light from the sun. Master Chin could not help but be impressed. The Tigers had never curled at his feet. All the animals of the forest visited her, except for the vipers, for as all the forest dwellers knew, the vipers befriended no one. Master Chin never spoke to her in all those years, not once. But he knew she was there. He knew her every move and expression. He was, in short, besotted with her, like any father with his daughter.

Then, one day, she came no more. Master Chin waited and waited, but no Ling Su. Finally, along about dusk, the chief, now old and bent, shuffled toward the master. The chief, tears streaming down his face, stood before the master.

Master Chin, whispered his first words in forty years, "Where is my daughter?"

"She is dead, master. Last night she found a pit viper that had been crushed in a landslide. She tried to free it and it bit her. She died without a sound. But, she smiled master, and I swear the moon stood still and the stars wept."

The master sat, still like an ancient mountain. Of course, he had known the exact instant she died. But he had hoped. One tear rolled down his cheek, and then another. "Now," he said to the old man in front of him, "now I know the meaning of love. And now, now I know the meaning of enlightenment." He bowed his head and wept silently. To this day the people in the forest say there is a mighty waterfall where he wept.

At dawn, Master Chin stood up, and bowed to the faithful old thief. "You have been a good and loyal friend. Stop thieving and start meditating." And with that the Master began to walk away into the forest.

Stunned, the chief, who was now secretly glad the master had not spoken in forty years, shouted, "Where are you going, Master?"

The Master said, "If I am to live as my Master Ling Su lived, then I must serve others."

And to this day, in that little country near China, there are

Ling Su orphanages, where all the children are taught the basics—Meditation, Stillness, and Love.

I would be one of those children.

Thank you,
> John Conley

Questioner: Master, is love human or divine or both? Is love a feeling? Is it an attitude? A belief? What is love, Master?

Baba Ram Jahn: I do not know how to describe love, child. It gets lost in words and I cannot find it, try as I might. The closest I can get is to say that we should let our minds be still and our hearts be love. All I know about love is that I love you!

August 28

Dear Friends:

In the jungle of my mind, there is a place I fear to tread; for there I will find all the lurking creatures of fear, hate, envy, greed, lust, and cowardice, all the things I have learned to loathe and avoid. If I go to that jungle, would I not become hateful and petty, resenting the success and happiness of others? Would I not lust after that which is not mine, and seek for that which should not be found? Would I not run from my duty and think only of myself?

I have lived like that before. And like all who have done so, I cast myself as a victim, which gave me the right to act in ways that are now repugnant to me. I hurt those I loved. And loved those I hurt. I acted selfishly, thinking only of myself. I behaved in ways that were wrong, both in the sight of God and man. So am I not right to avoid this dark place of my mind? Should I not flee it, as I would a ravenous beast, whose only desire is to devour and destroy me? Should I not hide and tremble?

The answer is gray. I would be arrogant to go into that jungle alone with a machete, hacking my way through the twisted vines of that dark place, challenging the beasts I met. No that would be foolish. Truly, I might be devoured. But this is what I have learned. As I reside in the Stillness, when these beasts cast their eyes upon me and seek to gain power over my actions, these very beasts I once feared and loathed are tamed by Stillness. When I bring these beasts into the power of Stillness, they flee as though they were rats.

Am I alone in having this dark jungle in my mind? No, of course not, I have much company. We all have this dark place, without exception. Some of us are more aware of it than others. Some of us have tamed more of the beasts than others. But all of us would do well to recognize its existence. The unknown enemy is the truly dangerous one. The unknown enemy lurks by the trail, waiting to attack the unsuspecting traveler.

But if we know where the enemy intends to set a trap, then we can circumvent that trap, and continue on our way unharmed. So do not fool yourselves, there lives a dark jungle in your mind. Do not fear it. Do not hide from it. But do not deny it. Do not deny its power to lure you from your spiritual path. Look closely at your thoughts, feelings, and actions. Do they reflect your highest ideals? If not, why not? Have you allowed yourself to get caught up in this jungle? Are you jealous of your friends? Angry at your wife? Mad at your children? Resentful of your manager? Are you practicing Stillness or fear?

If the answer is fear, do not berate yourself. Do not even berate the dark jungle of your mind. Rather, go into Stillness. Bask in the strength of Stillness. Allow the feelings from the jungle to arise as they will and surround them in the light of Stillness. These feelings, no matter how strong, will not last. If greed assails you, sit with it. If hate assails you, sit with it. If fear assails you, sit with it. Make the Stillness your refuge, your bastion against that part of yourself which would destroy all that you love.

Embrace the Stillness as though your very life depended upon it, for it does. Would you be happy? Embrace Stillness. Would you fulfill your destiny? Embrace Stillness. Would you be loving, kind, gentle, and all things good and true? Embrace Stillness. Embrace Stillness and hold on to it. Let the pain you find in the jungle be a wake-up call to return to Stillness.

Letters to My Friends

    I do not speak much of philosophy, mostly because I get confused. But here is the way I see myself. It is neither new nor original. But it helps me stay in Stillness. I believe I have a lower nature and a higher nature. These two comprise my ego. The lower nature is where the dark jungle grows. It is primitive and wild, violent and ruthless. We all have it. The higher nature is a meadow, often flooded with sunlight. It is a breeze on the ocean. It is here that I find the very human and wonderful feelings of love and compassion, of forgiveness and service. It is, in other words, my positive side, as the jungle is my negative side. Beyond both of these is my soul, my seat of choice. This is where I make a conscious choice to connect with Stillness. This is where I hear Stillness speak.

    And the Stillness speaks softly. It says do not be afraid. It says abide in me. It says love life and allow life to love you. It says hug and kiss. Be compassionate. It says I love you. You shall never die and you have never been born. As I am you, so you are me.

    And it says to watch the beasts in the dark jungle. Stillness says to be grateful for them, for had I not fled from them, I never would have run into the arms of Stillness.

    So, this is what Stillness says to me. Stillness will speak to you with a different voice, one perfect for you. So leave behind all that I have said, all of it, as you would leave a dark forest trail for a bright meadow, and hear the voice of your Stillness. Now.

Blessings,
    John Conley

John C. Conley

Questioner: Master, you look so sad. What is wrong, Master?

Baba Ram Jahn: Child. I am ill, very ill. I do not want to be ill. And I fear the fear of death.

Questioner: But, Master, have you not told me many times that there is no death? That though the body may decay, the soul lives forever? Have you not told me this many times?

Baba Ram Jahn: Yes, my daughter, many times I have told you this.

Questioner: Do you believe it, Master?

Baba Ram Jahn: Yes, child, I do.

Questioner: Then where is fear, Master?

Baba Ram Jahn: Fear? What fear? Let us live as though each breath is precious! We have no time for fear.

September 4

Dear Friends,

There is something you should know. Stillness is not for the faint-hearted. In practicing Stillness, everything that is not essential will be stripped away. Everything you want to hide will be revealed. All your fantasies will be dispelled. You can hide. You can cower. You can run. But Stillness, once you have touched it, will seek you out and rip apart your mind for you to see.

And this is what you will discover in your mind. You will be lacking. You will not be enough. That which you say you most desire will be out of your reach, for you will be too cowardly to grasp it. You will find that you say you want to practice Stillness, that you want to serve God and your fellow man, but you will find you do not; for these are just words, lacking in conviction, lacking in resolve and strength. You will find you are a weakling. You will find that if you really care, you will sink into despair.

After gazing into your mind, if you are fortunate, you will give up. You will surrender. And in that moment, you will be transformed. Stillness will permeate your life. You will be willing to face your own pain, your own suffering, your greed and deceit, for you will see that this very Stillness that has been chasing you down like a ravenous wolf pack chasing a deer is, indeed, the other face of you. Did you think that Stillness was all peace and joy? You were wrong. Stillness is the fire that hardens the clay, the furnace that molds the steel.

Yes, you will surrender, and in your surrender, you will find that the wolf pack wants to lick your wounds, feed and nourish you, and give you warmth. You will find the Stillness we have spoken of so often, sweet, gentle, and forgiving. You will find that you are the wolf.

But first the pain. If you are not willing to face your pain, leave off seeking Stillness. Do something else. Chase after wealth. Chase after the perfect job. Chase after the perfect mate and perfect children. Go to Cancun. Buy a vacation home. There is nothing wrong with this, except for one thing: pursuing these things will never make you happy, not now, not ever, especially not if Stillness has touched you. Because as you run after your dream life, Stillness will be whispering, "Empty, empty, this is all empty."

And then what? As the fire of Stillness hardens you into a bowl able to contain it, you will gather to yourself what you need in this world and you will be grateful. Your wife, the one you may have thought was drab, will suddenly be beautiful again. Your children will be perfect in your eyes because you will begin to see them with compassion. In the job you once hated, you will find meaning, as you become a blessing to all you meet.

Or perhaps you will change jobs. Your relationships may not work. Your children may be ungrateful. But you will see all this as an unfolding of life and you will not have to fix life.

There will be days when your bowl of Stillness will be full and all who come to you will drink from it. There will be other days when your bowl will seem empty, and those who come to you may think you are a hypocrite. It does not matter, for Stillness has you now as its willing partner. The journey has begun. It will never stop and it will never end. Each step is precious.

So, wherever you are on this endless unfolding path, do not be surprised if pain and fear arise. Do not be surprised if illness and injury come. Welcome them all in Stillness. Welcome them as gifts.

Letters to My Friends

Sit with them in Stillness. See what they have to teach you. They can be gentle teachers if you will allow them to teach gently.

But if you resist and fight these teachers, they will be neither gentle nor friendly. So, in Stillness, embrace all of life. Learn from it. Grow from it. Love it and you will transform your darkest moments into moments of exquisite Stillness.

This has been my experience. Over the past two years I have known more pain than I would like. Over the past two years I have suffered from injuries to my spine, and more recently from cancer. And I will tell you something. Nothing, nothing is more powerful than Stillness. Nothing brings more comfort and joy. Nothing lives within me as strongly as Stillness.

Thank you,
    John Conley

Questioner: Master, could you explain paradox to me?

Baba Ram Jahn: It has been said in the Bhagavad-Gita that two docks are better than one. For when the boat of the ego comes to shore, if it misses one dock, it will surely hit the other. And the docks, of course, represent the eternal Oneness of the Allness of the Isness.

Questioner: But, Master, I thought paradox meant that two separate, seemingly opposite things, can exist simultaneously and both be true.

Baba Ram Jahn: Child, child, this is what comes from reading too many spiritual books when one is not ready to assimilate the deeper truths. Was it not St. Paul who said that we see but through a glass darkly?

Questioner: Yes, I have heard that. But why was he looking through a glass? Was he looking for the pair of docks? And if it was a dirty glass, could he see them? Besides, I thought it was Peter who was a fisherman. Master, Master, where are you going?

Baba Ram Jahn: I am looking for a dock, daughter, a quiet dock. Any port in a storm, as the Upanishads say.

September 11

Dear Friends,

If I am full of hate, I will lead a hateful life. I will say hateful things and do hateful things. I will see a happy man and I will hate him. I will grumble angry words to his back. I will see a happy woman and I will hate her. I will think angry thoughts of her and throw them at her like stones. A child's smile will cause me to glare and a snarl will come to my lips. I will hate my country. I will hate my state. I will hate my town, my neighbors, my friends, my family. I will see compassion as weakness, and love as fear. I will see hate in all things and all things beautiful, I will hate.

And I will be trapped in a prison of my own making, a prison with no walls, yet one from which I cannot escape, as though it had walls of thick stone and bars of strong steel. Surely, I am not describing myself? Surely, I do not feel this way?

And most surely this is not us. We are spiritual seekers. We meditate and go to retreats. We read thick books. We engage in entertaining conversations about God. We do not lead hateful lives.

Or do we? How far is hate from contempt? How far is hate from irritation? I do not know. But I wonder. If we hold our president in contempt for going to war, are we not hating him? And if we hate him, are we not withholding from him both our spiritual love and our compassion in a time of great turmoil for both him and our country?

Conversely, if we hold the Islamic terrorists in contempt for their violence, and their intolerance of other faiths, are we not hating them? Should we not be holding them, too, in love and compassion?

Should we not hold them in Stillness, knowing that nothing is more powerful than Stillness?

These are big hates. What of little hates? What of our neighbor and his barking dog? If the dog irritates us with his midnight barking, when does the irritation turn to hate? When do we hate our neighbor for allowing his dog to bark?

We are, it sometimes seems, mad at the world for not being the way we want it to be. We hate it. We hate the pollution and the urban sprawl. We hate the poverty here in America, and we want somebody to blame. We hate violent crime and we fear our police, and fear is just another form of hate. We get irritated with snarls in the traffic. And jam jars that do not open easily elicit angry words. We fear fundamentalist Christians and wonder at their ignorance.

All these things, big and small, twine together, like a nest of snakes, and clutch our heart. The love is choked out of us and all the while we claim we are loving. We do not see the creep of little hatreds ruling our lives. Yet, these little hatreds make us tired of our life, tired of fighting, tired of trying to find some meaning.

There is an answer to this dilemma. We can allow all of our little hatreds, all of our big hatreds to be. Just allow them to be. Recognize them. Smile at them. And go into Stillness. We need not put any energy into trying to change ourselves, for we will fail. We will fail as though we were trying to jump from a high cliff and fly like a sparrow with rocks tied to our feet. We simply cannot change ourselves. But we can go into Stillness and there we will find the fundamental change we seek.

We can quit taking ourselves quite so seriously. We are small specks in a big universe. We do not have to cling to our beliefs as though our very lives depended on it, for they do not. We do not have to be right. Being right is highly overrated, is rarely needed, and is seldom right. More harm has been done out of the need to be right than from any other reason. Families are destroyed because of the need to be right. Nations fade into history because of the need to be right.

The right way to live is to not be concerned if we are right! We can relinquish hatred in all its sizes and disguises simply by embracing being wrong. We hate that which opposes us. But if we do not have to be right, then who is there to oppose us? Be wrong and laugh at it.

But how do we embrace being wrong? It is not as easy as it sounds. We have been taught from our earliest years that to be wrong is to die. We have been taught that to be wrong is to bring shame on ourselves and those we love. So how then do we become wrong?

There is only one way, of course. And that way is through Stillness, for in Stillness neither right nor wrong matters. What matters is Stillness. We may not agree with our president, but we send him love. We do not have to be right, and we do not have to make him wrong. We may abhor the actions of the terrorists. But we do not have to make them evil. We do, however, need to hold them in Stillness.

This is a choice we need to make. Do we respond with hate? Or do we respond with Stillness? Let Stillness be our guide in all our actions. Those actions we cannot perform in Stillness, we should avoid.

So now, let us close our eyes gently, breathe gently, and gently allow the Stillness to fill our awareness. Allow the Stillness to fill every fiber of our being with its gentleness. We will find that while we cannot change ourselves, Stillness can. And in Stillness we will take our stand.

Blessings,
    John Conley

Baba Ram Jahn: Questioner, my child, you look sad today. What is wrong?

Questioner: A friend of mine told lies about me, and this is the fourth time she has done it. Each time I trusted her not to lie about me and I forgave her and each time she lied again. I feel like a fool.

Baba Ram Jahn: Let me tell you a story. When I was a little boy, I found a baby rattlesnake that had been injured. I captured it. Took it home. And cared for it. My father told me not to trust a snake, for a snake was a snake and could not be trusted to be anything other than a snake. I did not believe him. Twice the snake bit me, and I got very sick. But I forgave the snake and got bit a third time. I learned my lesson and let the snake go. I forgave it, but I did not trust it.

Questioner: Yes Master, you are so wise. Thank you so much!

Baba Ram Jahn: Wait, daughter, where are you going? Why are you running?

Questioner: I am going to do just like you suggested, Master, and bite my friend. Then she will set me free!

September 18

Dear Friends,

My mother had a blue vase she loved very much. And I made a new friend. More about that later.

There is that which heals me, and there is that which destroys me. What heals me is sorrow, a sorrow so vast I cannot comprehend its depth, or its width, or its height. This sorrow calls me to compassion, for compassion is the fruit of sorrow. This sorrow fills my every muscle, my every bone. At times it seems overwhelming and I want to run, to hide, to never come into the light of day.

This sorrow is God calling me. But I have run all my life. Have I not fled into sex? Have I not fled into money? Have I not fled into drugs? Have I not fled into learning? Have I not fled into never finding and always seeking? Have I not fled into a secret misery that made me want to end my life knowing full well the devastation I would cause? I have done all these things and more.

I have fled sorrow, and thereby fled God. I wanted God to call me with joy, to call me with a tender voice into eternal bliss. Instead God called me into a sorrow so strong I can barely touch its edges.

Yet, now I know this sorrow leads me into compassion both for myself and others. But I will tell you something. At times, I do not want to join God in this sorrow, even if it leads to compassion. The sorrow hurts too much, and I have not yet completely learned the art of looking on suffering without suffering myself.

I see a snake in the road, twisting in agony after being hit by a car, and I feel its agony, even if only for a moment. I pray for it and say, "Poor snake. I hope you're reborn as a tiger in your next life, or an eagle."

This sorrow I feel makes me aware of how small I am, for I cannot stop the suffering, not that of the snake, nor my own. Nor can I stop your suffering. But I can be still. I can embrace the sorrow and not hide from it. Is that enough? I do not know, but often it is what I choose to do.

I become still, knowing I cannot right every wrong, knowing I cannot heal every wound, knowing I cannot comfort the wounded soldier or quiet the crying baby. I cannot reverse the waters or the winds. I cannot make each and every one of us compassionate. I cannot always be compassionate myself. But I can be still and I can embrace the sorrow and from it allow compassion to arise. And once compassion arises, I know Spirit can take it where it will, for compassion is a force that transcends all boundaries. I can rest in the knowledge that something much greater than I will dry the tears and bind the wounds. And this is a very good thing, for I, by myself, am alone and frightened. I am neither strong nor brave. But in Stillness, I have a measure of these things. This sorrow to me is the other face of God. This sorrow is why God chooses to know me. Without sorrow, I would be alone forever.

Yes, I would rather have bliss. But instead I find sorrow. Even in my meditation, I find sorrow. And in that sorrow, when I am very still, I find a gentleness, and a quiet joy greater than anything I have ever known. And it is this sorrow that causes me sometimes to love too much, to give too much, to care too much. But that is the price I pay for giving myself to sorrow.

It is also this sorrow that brings to light all my old hurt and pain, all my old fear and greed, and forces me to confront it. It is this sorrow that brings up my yearning to be loved, my need to be held,

Letters to My Friends

my desire to be comforted, and forces me to confront it. But as I face these old hurts and let them go, Stillness fills the empty spaces.

And the empty spaces are many and unexpected. I cried for my mother last night, probably for the first time since she died nearly forty years ago. I sobbed, all because I met a young woman at a meditation, who, for some unfathomable reason, reminded me of my mother. She had my mother's feel about her, with quick brown eyes that laughed one instant, and frowned the next. That was my mother. My mother died a long and painful death. I cared for her while my father worked. I will tell you I was too young to see her suffer so much for so long. It hurt too much. And I buried the pain deep. And then, last night, after the retreat, I cried. For once in my life I did not run from the sorrow of her death, and after the sorrow came Stillness.

So, my new friend, if you ever read these words, thank you. And, if reincarnation is true, as you believe, and if by chance you were my mother, I broke the vase, not Tony. I am really sorry I told a fib and got Tony in trouble, even though he deserved it. I'll be more careful next time.

Blessings,
    John Conley

Questioner: Master, last night I met a monk, and she said in order for me to become a monk, I would have to take a vow of celebrity. Why would a monk want to be famous?

Baba Ram Jahn: I think the monk meant a vow of celibacy, my child.

Questioner: And what is that?

Baba Ram Jahn: Actually, my daughter, the monk probably did mean celebrity. I'm sure of it. Now, why, is the question. Here is the answer. If one were famous, one would have many temptations to have a big ego. And if one had a big ego, one would have many opportunities to practice Stillness.

Questioner: That makes perfect sense, Master. But does that mean you have a big ego, for you practice Stillness more than anyone I know.

Baba Ram Jahn: Perhaps I do have a big ego, questioner. I do not think much about it. But I do know I have a big egg. A big chicken lays a big egg, and I am definitely a big chicken.

Autumn

September 25

Dear Friends,

    I am blessed beyond words. I have so many friends. Like many spiritual people, I grew up feeling different, feeling out of step, feeling as though somehow I did not quite belong to the human race. I still feel that way, of course! Nothing has changed about that aspect of my life. But now I have friends, and here is the ironic thing: I want very little from them, not even their love. This is not to say that I do not love my friends. I do. I love them dearly. I wish I could be with them more than I am. But in truth, the source of my joy is something much greater than my friends, something much greater than myself.

    Do you not think this is a cosmic joke? I am not sure it is funny, though. When I was growing up, I would have almost given my life to have friends. I felt so lonely, so sad. I spent many lonely days playing alone in the woods, making up games, exploring. I knew every trail and path in the forests near our house. I knew every swimming hole. I knew where every orchard and berry field was too. I smell even now the pungent odor of the fir boughs. I feel the cool grip of the water as it supported me. I can taste the sweetness of fresh cherries and I can see the juice running down my chin. Yet, more often than not, I experienced these delights alone. But in my aloneness, I became very quiet, very still. I think people thought I was a little odd. I suppose I was.

    But, in the Stillness, I grew a capacity to love deeply, to love strongly, to love so much that I think it scared people. My heart would open up to people, usually at unexpected moments, and I would want to hug them, to tell them I loved them. I learned very quickly, and often very painfully, that most people simply did not accept or understand this sort of love. I did not have the knowledge to deal with that sort of rejection and it drove me even deeper into myself. Even in church, demonstrations of love were deemed unacceptable. I went to the Evangelical Church of Hidden Feelings.

So, I grew up feeling alone. This thing I called God, the source, Buddha consciousness, call it what you will, became my friend. I thought about God everyday. Even after I discovered girls, I still thought about God, but not as much! God filled my heart. However, the loneliness was still there but as an undercurrent, tugging at my consciousness, but it did not hurt until I thrust my consciousness into it.

So now I have friends, but I want very little from them. No, that is not true either. I have friends, and what I want from them is for them to allow me to love them. I want them to understand and accept me when I say, "I love you." I want them to understand when I give them long hugs and my heart melts. So, in reality, the little I ask from my friends is much more than a little. But I have some very good friends.

Here is a little story about love. All day long I listen to sad stories, stories of pain and discouragement, tempered with courage. One elderly lady today said, "I cannot put him in a home, even though my children think I should. He's no trouble. He doesn't remember who I am or who he is. And I can't leave him alone for a minute. But he's no trouble." She was speaking of her husband of forty-seven years.

Was that God's love? Was that human love? Is there a difference between the highest expression of human love and the pouring forth of God's love? I do not think so. I think God bows to us in humility because our love has so much to overcome. God is awed by this woman's love, of that I am sure, in the same way that we are awed by the accomplishments of our children.

I said I only want my friends to allow me to love them. But I wonder if even that is too much. Perhaps I can only love them completely when I want nothing from them. Ironically, this is why I believe the love of God is absolute. God, despite what we have been taught, demands nothing from us.

I know that I love you, even when I am clumsy, even when I am confused, even when I stumble over my words. My feelings sometimes flow so strongly that directing them takes all the strength I have. I know that I care deeply. I know, above all, that when I love, Stillness is manifesting through me. Stillness chooses me, chooses you, as vehicles of love, regardless of our faults.

If we stumble in our expression of God, if we say the wrong thing, or even sometimes do the wrong thing, Stillness will still manifest through us as love. This is the divine union that we all seek. To God, we are all one; therefore, let us be still and know that we are God.

Blessings,
    John Conley

Baba Ram Jahn: Daughter, I have a koan for you. How many buds could a Buddha bud if a Buddha could bud buds?

Questioner: Are they big buds or little buds? Is it spring or summer? Are they getting plenty of water and nourishing food? Is there any frost? Are there plenty of bees? Is Buddha a careful gardener?

Baba Ram Jahn: My child, this is a koan, the answer must be found in silence!

Questioner: So, Baba Ram Jahn, my Master, you do not know the answers to my questions?

Baba Ram Jahn: I shall invoke a noble silence, as did the Buddha.

Questioner: Then, Master, that must mean we are going for a walk. But, please, no more of these silly koans. I am still thinking about the sound of one hand slapping. Remember? You asked me about that one too? What was he slapping? And why? Was he mad? And why do I think the hand was a man, Master? That is simple. A woman would not lose her hand! She has too much work to do. And, Master, I really enjoy this noble silence of yours. It becomes you. Shall we talk some more?

October 2

Dear Friends,

    I thought I was born to suffer, and suffer I did. For many years that was my fate, and I did not seem able to escape it, no matter how sustained and desperate my effort. But that is past me. And now, with each breath I take, I see the face of God. With each breath I take, I know a peace that passes understanding. With each breath I take, I rest in Stillness. How did this miracle happen?
    I do not understand it completely. But I will try to explain it. I gave up seeking answers. I must have read thousands of books on spiritual growth. I had no choice, for to be a seeker was also my fate. Yet, the lessons I learned were always short-lived. Always, without fail, I would slip back into anger and fear, my questions unresolved. Are we saved by grace? Maybe, maybe not. Are we saved by our own efforts? Maybe, maybe not. Is all that I experience an illusion? Maybe, maybe not. Seeking answers to questions such as these was a disease of mine.
    But one day, something I cannot totally explain happened. At Still Meadows near the soft ripple of the Clackamas River, I sat with a small group of fellow seekers listening to Karen McPhee speak. I went to listen to her because she had studied with Eckhart Tolle, author of *The Power of Now*. And I had been studying *The Power of Now* daily for nearly two years.
    Karen directed us toward the flow of eternal, unchanging Stillness within, and she said, "When thoughts arise, smile at them, wave at them, love them, and return to the Stillness." And suddenly, there I was, a part, a small part of that eternal Stillness and all the

Letters to My Friends

while my thoughts raced by. But it was as though someone else were thinking them. And I was free, once and for all, free. I knew then and there I was more than my thoughts. I was the experience of Stillness also.

After several decades of meditation, I finally—a very slow learner—had learned this fundamental truth. I am not my thoughts only. I am the Stillness within, eternal and unchanging. And what is more, I learned both of these aspects of myself could exist simultaneously.

I loved Karen then, and I love her now. She does not like to be called a teacher, but she is. Her words freed me from dark places. Also, like all true teachers I know, she does not want to be set on a pedestal, and truly I am not putting her on one. The divine in me recognizes the divine in Karen. But the child of the Spirit, this human, transient being named John, is grateful to her.

Since that day with Karen, there have been days, many days to be truthful, when I have been lost almost completely in my thoughts. But always, always, I sensed the Stillness resting beneath, waiting for me to return. And then there have been other days when the Stillness was a roaring river. My thoughts would slow to a trickle and the flow of Stillness would carry me away. And, occasionally, my thoughts would stop all together. I do not try to dictate my experience.

And now, with each breath I take, I see the face of God. With each breath I take, I know a peace that passes understanding. With each breath I take, I rest in Stillness. Does this mean I am always happy? No. Does this mean I am perfect? No. Does this mean I never make mistakes? No. But it does mean the Stillness is always there, always, just a breath away. With each breath we are offered a choice: Stillness or something less than Stillness.

This is your choice. Feel this Stillness in your heart. Feel the awakening of this Stillness in your mind. And know that always you are this Stillness. As you inhale, feel the power of your Stillness rising up from your belly through your heart and throat and into your face. As you exhale out, feel the warmth flowing from your heart as it enlivens every fiber of your body. With every breath, we are given this choice. With every breath, we can unfold as a rose of awakening. *Om, Shanti, Shanti, Shanti.*

Blessings,
    John Conley

Letters to My Friends

Questioner: Master, I have been thinking about my life and what I should do with it.

Baba Ram Jahn: Thinking is highly overrated, daughter. Many years ago I entered the void and left thinking behind. Words happen. Teaching happens. But this is without effort or volition on my part.

Questioner: Does dressing happen too, Master?

Baba Ram Jahn: Well, yes, daughter. All things simply unfold.

Questioner: That would explain why your socks are mismatched. And why your hair is sticking straight up in the air like a tuft of grass. The divine is very mysterious.

Baba Ram Jahn: True, daughter. It took no thought on my part to dress this way. The fashion in which I dress simply unfolded.

Questioner: Yes, Master, I have no doubt of that. And that is because you follow the divine masculine. I think I will follow the divine feminine!

Baba Ram Jahn: Nonsense, child, the masculine divine has excellent fashion sense, a sense every bit as well developed as that of the divine feminine.

Questioner: Yes, Baba Ram Jahn. By the way, Master, your pants are unzipped.

October 9

Dear Friends,

Few words more beautiful have ever been spoken in any language. Here is the Apostle Paul speaking of love:

> *If I speak in the tongues of men and of angels, but have not love, I am only a resounding gong or a clanging cymbal. If I have the gift of prophecy and can fathom all mysteries and all knowledge and I have a faith that can move mountains, but have not love, I am nothing. If I give all I possess to the poor and surrender my body to the flames, but have not love, I gain nothing.*
>
> ——1 Corinthians 13:1-3

> *Love is patient, love is kind. It does not envy, it does not boast, it is not proud. It is not rude, it is not self-seeking, it is not easily angered, it keeps no record of wrongs. Love does not delight in evil but rejoices with the truth. It always protects, always trusts, always hopes, always perseveres. Love never fails. But where there are prophecies they will cease; where there are tongues, they will be stilled; where there is knowledge, it will pass away. For we know in part and we prophesy in part, but when perfection comes, the imperfect disappears.*
>
> —1 Corinthians 13:4-10

I remember reading these words as a young man and feeling so inspired. Yet, I also felt forlorn. How, I wondered, could I ever be so loving? For was I not impatient, unkind, easily angered, and envious? Yes, I was. And, in truth, I often still am.

But there is hope, for the Stillness that resides in me, the Stillness that gives life to all of us, manifests in goodness. Therefore, I would add this to what the Apostle Paul said—be still. Be still and be loving. Be still and be kind. Be still and be patient. All of these traits are ours in Stillness.

But if you seek to strive to be a better person of your own accord, know that you are destined to fail. And it is not just I who say this. I repeat only what I have heard from those much wiser than I. Read the words of Christ in the Gospel of Luke. Read the words of Krishna in the Bhagavad-Gita. Read the words of Buddha in the Dhammapada. Read these words and you will know unless we touch that which I call Stillness, we will fail, no matter how valiant our efforts, no matter how determined our step, no matter how unflagging our courage.

If we touch not Stillness we will fail. We will fail to touch that which is ourselves, our eternal, abiding, unchanging selves. This self of which I speak is mightier than the mightiest wind, yet more gentle than the kiss of a mother. This self of which I speak is more magnificent than the grandest of galaxies in far distant space, yet more common than a fallen leaf.

Would you be saved? Would you find your salvation? Would you escape from this mundane world? Then enter into Stillness. The path into Stillness spreads before us like a broad boulevard, lined with great trees and fragrant flowers. Yet we do not see it. Would you find Nirvana and live there for eternity? Then enter into Stillness. Would you enter the mindfulness of the monk? Then enter into Stillness, for there you will find eternity. You will find yourself. Would you lead a simple life, full of love, full of laughter, full of the joy of good friends? Then enter into Stillness. For it is in Stillness that we find that which we seek.

There is a peace that truly passes understanding, and is but one breath away. Read a thousand books and this peace will yet be a breath away. Find the wisest teacher and this peace will yet be one breath away. Embrace miraculous powers and be known throughout the world as a renowned teacher, and this peace will yet be one breath away. For how can God be distant? Can that which is you flee from you? Can that which is you hide? Can that which is you separate itself from you, even for one moment? No, no, and no.

This Stillness cares nothing for our accomplishments. It cares nothing for our learning. It cares nothing for our wealth or power. It cares only that we experience it as ourselves—now, today—not tomorrow, not yesterday. It cares that we give and receive love. It cares that we know once and for all that we are never alone, not even in the darkest night of our soul.

One breath away, in one little breath away resides this Stillness. Close your eyes. Draw a breath. There is a magic in this as ancient as humankind. Feel the flow of life as it rises from your belly to your heart to your throat to your eyes. This feeling of life is the edge of Stillness. You are now with each breath awakening. With each breath you are now putting your awareness into Stillness, and that Stillness will welcome you now and forever. It is that easy. It is that glorious.

But it must be done now. There is no other time. The time for waiting is past. We are called to enter Stillness now. For time grows short for our precious planet. Is that not obvious? Our forests are dying. Our oceans are sick. And we kill each other. Yes, the time for Stillness is now. Those of us who have touched Stillness must point the way to Stillness, however incomplete and weak we may feel. This pointing does not have to be big. We do not have to preach

Letters to My Friends

from the mountaintops. A kind word will do. A smile. A helping hand. Laughter and love, these will heal the world in Stillness.

So, with the Apostle Paul, let us bring love to the world.

Blessings,
John Conley

> Questioner: Master, if I fell down a cliff and was stranded, would you come to my aid?
>
> Baba Ram Jahn: I would fly to you, child, on angel wings.
>
> Questioner: What if a big bear were on the ledge with me? Would you help me then?
>
> Baba Ram Jahn: Yes, my child. I would tickle the bear until it sneezed and ran away.
>
> Questioner: But what if a big snake crawled down to me? What would you do then?
>
> Baba Ram Jahn: I would crawl faster than the snake, and ask him very politely to leave.
>
> Questioner: And what, Baba Ram Jahn, if I did something I knew was wrong? Would you love me then?
>
> Baba Ram Jahn: When I am perfect, daughter, that is when I will stop loving you, and there is no hope of my being perfect.
>
> Questioner: And why is that, Master?
>
> Baba Ram Jahn: Because there is room only for one perfect person in each household, and that perfect person is you, child.

October 16

Dear Friends,

There was an old draft horse named John who for many years had pulled his wagon faithfully. Yet this old horse longed to be free. He wanted to run with the mustangs in the wild mountains to the west. He looked at them longingly, but always, he bowed his head, leaned into the traces, and plodded onward.

The mountain horses ran to India. They studied horse meditation with the gurus there. They raised their kundalini and practiced yoga. They came home with wonderful stories and became teachers of the other horses and taught mantras.

But the old draft horse, he had no mantra. "I am boring. I pull my family. I could live a more exciting life if I was not afraid." He thought about this often. "But how could I ever leave my family? That is too high of a price to pay for freedom. And my friends," he thought, "the horses that pull beside me, they depend on me. I cannot leave. What would they do if I did not pull my share?"

As the years passed, the horse grew old, but he kept pulling. He knew his family needed him to pull the wagon over rough roads to the market where they could sell their goods. And he pulled them to church on Sundays. He pulled when he felt sick. He pulled when his hooves grew sore and when his back ached with the strain. He pulled when every morning became a struggle to walk out of his stall and face a new day.

Yes, he pulled and he pulled. He sometimes felt sad at his mundane life. He had done nothing great or wonderful. Then one day he passed an old mare grazing at the side of the road, where she daintily nibbled at the long stalks of early summer grass. She had seen many years. Hard work had swayed her back and her legs bowed in with the knees almost touching. And she said, "Say the name of God even once with total love and your sorrows will disappear like grass in the dry heat of summer."

"Who," he neighed, "are you?"

She smiled at him with kind eyes and a smile that lit the world. "My name is Krishna Das." The old draft horse snorted and trudged on and on until he reached the village. "What kind of silly name is that?" he thought. But then he thought, "Who is this God I should name? Where do I find this God?" He snorted again and shook his head. His thick mane almost bristled. He had no time for silly women.

The next day, as he again pulled the wagon, he again passed the mare as she rolled in the grass. The draft horse could smell the crushed sweetness of the grass as the breeze whiffed it to his velvet nose. "Did you," she asked, "Say the name of God?"

"No! I did not. Where do I find this God?" The draft horse whinnied, feeling surprised at himself for asking. But he was tired and lonely. His heart hurt and he longed for rest.

"Do not seek for God. Say only the name of God. There is nothing to seek, nothing to find, nothing to do, nowhere to go. Say the name of God only and in that Stillness you will know freedom."

"But what name should I say?" the draft horse bellowed, tossing his head and stamping his feet like a colt.

"That is very easy to answer," said the old mare. "Say the name of Jesus or Krishna or Rama. These three gave themselves up to love. Say their names until you find the one true name of God that is yours and yours alone."

"And what is that name?" But the old mare had fallen asleep. The draft horse shook his head and plodded onward yet once again to the village. But he said the name of God. Oh, yes, again and again, day after day, month after month, year after year, he said the name of God. He never saw the mare Krishna Das in all that time. But he said the name of God in good health and in bad, in good times and in bad. He said the name of God until the name of God said itself.

Hare Rama, Hare Rama, Rama, Rama, Hare Hare.

Hare Krishna, Hare Krishna, Krishna, Krishna, Hare, Hare.

Hare Jesus, Hare Jesus, Jesus, Jesus, Hare, Hare.

He grew old and he kept chanting. And one day he collapsed. He fell over and was too tired to get up. His legs kicked feebly. But he kept chanting. His family climbed down from the wagon, and in their faces he saw God. His harness mates gathered around him and in their faces he saw God. He looked over the fields and the valley, and at the village in the distance and he saw God. He looked at the mountains and the wild mustangs and he saw God.

His family cried. His harness mates cried. And he saw God shed tears. And then as his tired eyes dimmed, he saw the mare Krishna Das.

"Teacher," he whispered, "will you now tell me the true name of God?"

She smiled, "What is your name?"

Surprised, he said, "John."

"What is your name?" she asked again.

"John."

"What is your name?"

Letters to My Friends

The old horse smiled and whispered one last time, "John." And God died.

Blessings,
John Conley

Questioner: If, Baba Ram Jahn, my Father, you could teach me but one thing, what would that be?

Baba Ram Jahn: I know very little, my daughter, but of the little I know, I know this best. "Dance, for that which we seek is within us. Sing, for that which we seek is within us. Laugh, for that which we seek is within us." And this, child, above all is what I would say. "Love, for that which we seek is within us." And that, my fairy princess, is all I know.

October 23

Dear Friends,

    To those who suffer, know there is an end to suffering. To those who fear, know there is an end to fear. To those who cry, know there is an end to tears. To those who grieve, know there is an end to grieving. And to those who despair, know that there is an end to despair, for all things end, except for one, and that is Stillness.

    Know too that laughter ends, as does happiness. Know that your accomplishments will perish and your body will wither. Your loved ones will die. And you yourself will know illness. To deny this is to deny life. All things change, except for one and that one is God.

    And where does this God live? In the sky? In a holy book? In our hearts? Rather we should ask where God is not. For God is everywhere, in all things, at all times. God breathes life into all creatures and also into the stones. Yet God is beyond our comprehension, beyond our explanation, beyond our words. Our words are but the babbling of infants. No matter how glorious the words, how insightful, they are still nothing but words. Everything we read is wrong. Everything we learn is wrong. Everything we know is wrong. All are but a dim reflection of the truth.

    But, even though we cannot understand the infinite, we can taste it. We can touch it. We can see it. We can smell it. We taste it in the salt air. We touch it on the soft muzzle of a newborn colt. We see it in the exquisite beauty of a raindrop. We smell it in the fragrance of a rose. God is all around us. And we breathe God with every breath. We breathe Stillness with every breath. Truly, our awakening is but one breath away.

Just under our breath, Stillness resides, waiting for us to notice its infinite reach, waiting for us to be still, so that we can become Stillness itself. This is the joy we all seek, the joy we have sought throughout our entire lives.

We can read a thousand books and be no nearer to Stillness. We can engage in a thousand learned talks and be no closer to Stillness. We can travel to the far ends of the earth and seek out the wisest teachers and be no closer to Stillness.

How can we get closer to something that never left us? How can we find that which is not lost? Where do we look for ourselves? We are that which we seek. We are that for which we yearn. We are Stillness.

But if you must seek, then seek no further than beneath your breath. Peek behind your breath and you will see Stillness. The breath that infuses you with life, this is our experience of Stillness.

The joy I experience is beyond anything I imagined possible, and it arises from Stillness. This breath of which I speak is life itself. But there are also days when I feel as though I am rummaging through a cluttered closet. I see an old resentment and pick it up like an old photo and relive it in every detail. And there, in the corner behind the shoes, I see a sock full of jealousy. And over here, by the broom, is a dustpan full of anxiety, the gnawing kind that nags and nags and nags and never goes away. But always, always, no matter how far I stray, I come back to the Stillness.

I come back not because I am saintly, but because I am tired of hurting others, and tired of being hurt myself. There have been many times in my life when I longed to leave this earth, and I do not mean by killing myself. I simply wanted to leave. The pain and confusion were simply too much to bear. But now I have Stillness. And the most amazing thing has happened. Even when I am sad, I feel a strong current of joy.

When I was a little boy, I rarely listened to my mother. Those who know me well will not be surprised by this revelation! An abandoned well lurked near our house, hidden in the blackberry bushes, and my mother told me again and again never to go near it. So, of course, I did, and I fell into it. I stood on the rotten boards that covered the well and they broke. I fell perhaps twenty feet and landed on a pile of rubble. Fortunately the well was long dry or I would have drowned. How long I stayed there, I do not remember. It could not have been more than a day. But I remember this. I was unafraid. I felt surrounded by a calmness, by a Stillness. As it was getting dark, I remember looking up at a circle of fading light and seeing a face peer down at me. I think it may have been a neighbor. I do not know. I remember feeling not relief, but a sadness that I was leaving that still space. Had I known what life had in store for me, I might have stayed in that hole!

I spent many, many years after that trying to find that Stillness and not finding it, not finding it because it was there with me all the time, and all I needed to do was listen. And finally, when I did listen, I heard the Stillness and the Stillness became my song, a song I sing to all who will listen.

Blessings,
    John Conley

Questioner: Baba Ram Jahn, I met a monk who told me I must overcome my ego to be enlightened. Is this true?

Baba Ram Jahn: There are, daughter, many who say that it is so. These people have an angry inner beagle. Their beagle snarls and barks, and bites everything that moves. So naturally, they view their inner beagle as an enemy that has to be overcome. But there are others who view their inner beagle as a cute fuzzy mutt that sometimes howls at the moon or pees on the rug. These people view their beagle as a companion on the road to enlightenment.

Questioner: No, Father, I said ego. It is a psychological term having to do with our sense of self.

Baba Ram Jahn: Of course, child, there are those who also speak of the inner igloo. The discussions about these things are endless. Let us go for a walk and chant the names of God. Did you know that the ancient ones say that if we chant the name of the divine even once with perfect love, we will become enlightened?

Questioner: Yes, Father, let us walk and let us sing. But let us avoid nasty beagles and cold igloos. I think you are right. Who needs these things?

October 30

Dear Friends,

    I walked to the top of a high hill, and there spread before me, in the valley below, I saw God. I saw God in the stream as it soared its way through the green grass bending gently to the music of the wind. I saw God in the red leaves of the vine maples as they winked and sparkled at the sun. I saw God in the endless blue sky, a sky so vast that the distant eagle flew as small as a sparrow. I saw God in the rough bark of the fir tree, and in the little brown snake at my feet. I saw God in the green moss on the boulders that adorned the stream like a necklace of raw emeralds. I saw God in the decaying wood of a stump that was the world to a family of ants. I saw God in me. I saw God in you. I saw God in everyone and in everything.

    And then I walked down the hill and into the valley and back into my life. And there I saw God in my daughter, Emma. I saw God in Joan. I saw God in the pile of dirty dishes, and in the tub of dirty motor oil. I saw God in an old pair of shoes. I saw God in my neighbor and in the clerk at the hardware store. God peeked out at me from everywhere at all times. When my daughter Helen rolled her eyes at one of my jokes, the eyes of God rolled. When my daughter Hannah smiled at me, I knew the love of God in my heart, and this love pierced so deep it hurt. When I sang, I heard God. When I spoke, I heard God. And God heard me.

    I saw God in the eyes of my friends. I saw God in the sorrow of my friends. I saw God in the laughter of my friends, and in the anger. I saw God in the unwashed beggar on the street corner. I saw God everywhere and in all things. And I wanted to hide.

I wanted to hide because God called to me to serve, called to me to be more than I am, called to me to forget who I think I am and be something more, something much more. And I wanted to hide. I wanted to run and hide and never think or say the word God again.

The trees called to me to serve them, to save them from the ravages of ruthless progress. The stream called to me to keep it free of the filth of progress. My children called to me to love them and care for them; to be a better, more loving father than I am. My friends called to me to ease their pain, to help them understand their suffering. The beggar called to me to feed him, to not avert my head in fear and shame.

Everywhere I turned I heard God calling, "John, serve me. Serve that which I am." And I felt too weak, too small, and too ignorant. I know very little. I read thick books and shake my head in wonderment that so much could be written about what cannot be explained in words. I study complicated forms of meditation with many difficult techniques to master and I wonder how the means became the end. I have but a little knowledge. I am weak and afraid. How can I serve? How can I help?

And then I remembered this. God is everywhere in all things at all times. I need do nothing but remember that and live my life. We touch God in the smallest of ways, with a smile, with a laugh. There is no need to do great things. Simply do the little things well, for that in itself is greatness.

When you read a story to your little boy at night, read it with all your attention. When you kiss your husband good night, kiss him as though it is the last kiss you will know. When you laugh, laugh hard. When you smile, let your eyes twinkle. When you wash dishes, sing and splash. See what floats and what sinks. Greet all of life with joy, for joy is life and life is joy.

John C. Conley

    Greet suffering with a warm heart, for often this will be all that you have to give. A warm heart heals pain and chases away anger. There will be things in this life that will rip your heart from your body and trample it as though it were dirt. Bloody children must be met with a warm heart. Grieving mothers must be met with a warm heart. Fathers whose hearts cry must be met with a warm heart. Those who commit crimes, who destroy the defenseless and innocent, must be met with compassion, even while you gird yourself against them.

    We find God in the living of life, for God is not hidden. We need seek nothing. We serve God by living life with courage and joy, by following our heart in all things. God wants nothing from us, not our worship, not our faith, nor our belief. God does not want us to convert the heathen or save the pagans. God does not want us to make holy wars on our neighbors. God does not even want our love. God asks only one thing from us and that is to serve one another with dignity and grace, to be gentle and kind, to hold each other in our sorrow and to praise each other in our joy. This is all God asks from us. But God does not demand. And if we give this to God, our lives then will be full and happy, whether we are rich or poor, whether we are in poor health or good health. Our lives will be full and happy, for our source will be that which cannot be tarnished or destroyed.

    My word for God is Stillness. And I will return to Stillness now, for when I am still I have found God and when I have found God I have found Stillness. But this Stillness is not the Stillness of a silent dawn. This Stillness can be full of laughter, music, shouting, and noise. Horns honk in this Stillness. Kids play tag in this Stillness. Mothers coo in this Stillness. Boys yell and tackle each other in this Stillness. Fathers cuss in this Stillness when the wrench slips and the knuckles get skinned.

Letters to My Friends

    This Stillness is nothing special. It is there, just beneath the surface of our minds, at all times in all places. We need do nothing special to find it. But because our minds are so noisy, a simple vehicle to enter into the Stillness is a good thing. We can sing the name of God. We can chant. We can allow the kundalini to rise. We can sit quietly and follow our breath. We can listen to music. We can walk. We can watch our thoughts and feelings rise. I do all of these things, but they are only vehicles to Stillness not Stillness itself. I do not concern myself overly much with the inner workings of these techniques. That they, in their most simple forms, take me where I want to go is enough for me.

    And where is it I go? I go to a place far away yet near, a place of joy and peace, a place of laughter, a place where love emanates like sun rays from the sun, and that place is here with me now and always, just a breath away.

Your friend,
    John Conley

Questioner: Master, I just read a book that was 343 pages long and it said I had to do all the meditations exactly as explained and in the order outlined or I would never awaken. I am doomed, Master, for I could not even do one exactly as explained.

Baba Ram Jahn: Much has been written about very little, daughter, as though the understanding of the thing is the experience of the thing. It is as though we think if we understand the structure, for example, of the breath, we experience the breath itself.

Therefore, daughter, a book with many steps may be book with many steps to nowhere.

Questioner: But Master, you love to write. I know you do. Now I am even more confused.

Baba Ram Jahn: Daughter, there is but one thing I take seriously, and that is Stillness, and there is but one step to Stillness. Everything else I write simply points to Stillness. And can you tell me, dear questioner, what that step is right now?

Questioner: Oh Master, is this a test? I love your tests. They are always so easy. Right now, in this moment, our love for each other is that step. Oh, Master, I do so love being right. Perhaps, though, Baba Ram Jahn, if you want your teachings to be widely known you should write a book with many steps, one like *How to Awaken in 30 Days!* or *A Thousand Steps to Spiritual Success* . . . or *Step into Enlightenment the Baba Ram Jahn Way* or . . .

November 6

Dear Friends,

    I do not know if anything I believe is true; but true or not true, it matters little. I only know when I am still and when I am not. All my beliefs about karma, about heaven and hell, about the nature of God, they are just that—beliefs, nothing more. If we have too many things that we know to be true, truths that we must defend, then we risk blocking the very thing we seek—Stillness.

    Truth belongs to the infinite web of life. All things return to the web, for it is the web that brought us to this moment in time. My web, and yours, extends backwards to the beginning of time and forward to the end of time. It connects me with God and with all else that exists. I am ancient. I am young.

    This web of which I speak is not a theory to me. It is Truth. I see it in my heart. I see it as a vast shimmering carpet of silver strands stretching on forever and ever. I am this web, for it cannot be divided; and that is the illusion, that it can be divided. This web moves in time as one continuous whole, and because of that, I never act alone. Indeed, I cannot.

    I am simply unfolding with the rest of creation. My every thought, feeling, and action is an unfolding of this web. All of creation manifests through me. I am not alone. I am not making decisions and taking actions in a void. I am not directing the universe, or even my part in it. Life, from the perspective of the web, has nothing to do with choice. I simply flow with the web. I am the wind. I do not choose where to go. I am the rain. I do not choose when to fall. I am the sun. I do not choose when to shine. Yet, I act as though I make choices. And that is the illusion. I make no choices. Not even the web makes choices. It simply is.

This means, then, that at any given moment, everything is exactly as it should be. I literally need do nothing to change the web. Indeed, I cannot. And that again is the illusion. I believe that through my thoughts I can influence the web. This is silly, childish. I am, as are all things, the unfolding of this web.

This then, this web, is what we call grace. We cannot understand it, but we can see it. It is why one man is born with a thirst for God, and another is born with a thirst for riches. It is why one woman thinks first of helping others and another thinks first of helping only herself. The desire is the same in all cases. But the object of the desire is different. This too is from the web. Grace is why some seek Stillness, and others do not. Grace is what reaches out and grabs our hearts and drags us into Stillness. Grace is why others laugh at Stillness.

Does this mean then that we should resign ourselves to our fate, knowing that it is ordained in the intricate strands of the web of life? I do not know. But I believe that once through grace we have touched Stillness, we have no choice but to seek it. Once Stillness has touched us, it will leave such a sweetness in our souls, we will struggle to find it and learn from it, for we will want that sweetness to abide like a rock and not wither like an autumn rose. Yet, even though the longing for Stillness is ordained in the web, even though I have no choice, in the end, I must act as though I do.

I must act as though my every choice makes a difference. And, who knows, perhaps it does. Perhaps choice is hidden in the web in ways I cannot see or understand. And if choice is ordained, then I have no choice but to say this once again: With every breath we take, we can enter into Stillness. We can know God. We can begin to flow effortlessly with the web as it unfolds. We must act with

Letters to My Friends

courage, faith, and love, for that too is the web waiting for itself to unfold. And this too, this belief in a web unfolding, is nothing more than a belief. In the end, all I know is Stillness.

Blessings,
   John Conley

Baba Ram Jahn: Today, daughter, I will speak of aardvarks, hens, and peanut butter.

Questioner: And why, Master, would you do that?

Baba Ram Jahn: Because, child, if the divine is divine, we should see the divinity in the aardvarks, hear the divinity in the cackle of the hen, and taste the divinity in the peanut butter.

Questioner: Yes, Baba Ram Jahn, this is very wise. But could we not taste the divinity in a fried chicken? And could we not forget the aardvark altogether and substitute a baked potato? And, as for the peanut butter, we will make that into cookies for dessert. We must be practical in our spiritual path, Master. I think the path to enlightenment does not need to be hard. That is why we have divinity fudge. But have you ever heard of divinity aardvarks, Master? I do not think so!

Baba Ram Jahn: Daughter, I despair of you. And after all I have taught you. You forgot thick, black coffee with lots of cream and sugar. Surely coffee is divine. And we must remember to suffer, just a little bit, so that we do not feel guilty!

November 13

Dear Friends,

The sun rises and sets and the moon rises and sets, as though they were the beginning and end of a tail. The seasons come and go, each in its turn, always following the same order. The flock of crows outside my window sleeps at night and awakes early in the morning. They talk to each other in raucous voices filled with glee. The raccoons, the babies scurrying after the mother, come out at night and drink. The mother chits at her babies when they stop to wrestle. The cats in our house sleep by day and sleep by night. They are kings and queens, without, as far as I can tell, a worry in the world.

Everything around me unfolds effortlessly. Yet, here am I, worried about tomorrow, worried about today, worried about yesterday. There are yet days when fear grips me with its strong talons like a hawk with its prey. Perhaps the talons do not grip me for the full day, not anymore at least, but grip me they do. Thoughts of work, money, and children clatter in my mind and make demands. My wife clatters there too, making demands she would never make outside my mind.

Those talons of the mind can grip hard. I question myself. Has my life been worthwhile? Is it my ego that asks this question? Do I have an ego? If all is one, how can I be two? What do I need to do to make my life worthwhile? Am I too timid? Should I jump into the stream of life, rather than stick my toe in to test the waters? Maybe I have jumped in and I only think I have stuck my toe into the surface.

These are not necessarily bad questions, not if they are asked once or twice a month, or in extreme cases, once or twice a week. But there are times when I feel like these questions echo in my mind again and again and again. And my efforts to answer them only arouse more questions, which in turn demand more attention and give rise to yet more questions; ones which cannot now or ever be answered, but still I try.

And then I remember to unfold, to simply unfold. I remember the Stillness of the deep waters underneath the surface storms. I remember I am that Stillness, and I stay there, perhaps for a second or two, or a minute or two, or an hour or two, or even a day or two. And then something demands my attention. Perhaps my daughter feels overwhelmed with her homework, and she turns to me for help two hours before an assignment is due. Or perhaps, a friend at work is mad at another friend at work, and they both turn to me for help. Or the pilot light on the furnace is out. Or one of the cats has been in a fight with a skunk. And before you know it, I am fixing and advising. Or perhaps, the toilet is leaking. I am feeling alarmed and concerned.

Come with me on a magical journey into the bathroom. The toilet is leaking and the talons of my mind grip hard. Yes, I am working on the toilet, wishing all the while I was hiking in the mountains, and feeling bad because I am not here now in the present moment with the beloved toilet. I remember the Chinese are the newly arriving economic power. How will this impact my life, my country?

And speaking of the Chinese, who was that actor in the movie about the Japanese? Tom Somebody. Why does my wife think he is so cute? Why do my daughters think he is so cute? There is no explaining taste. I am supposed to be still! What will Ram Dass think? What will Eckhart Tolle think? Who cares? For heavens sake, I have never met either of these men, even though they are like book ends in the library of my spiritual life.

I am supposed to be present! I am supposed to be here now!

I have to pause and meditate. But no, if I do that, the bathroom will flood, because I just broke the water valve! So, now we are back to water, but this time it is flowing from a pipe and spreading on the floor. And suddenly I am very present. I become absorbed, totally absorbed, in stopping the unwanted flow of water. And as I am trying to stick a pencil in the little copper tube from which the water squirts into my face, it occurs to me that I was never not present. All my thoughts, all my feelings, all the endless chattering of my mind, that too is a part of Stillness, but my conditioned mind tells me it is not. I have learned to define Stillness. This is it and this is not.

But, wait a minute, does this mean I am still, that I am present, even when I think I am not? Yes, that is exactly what it means. Everything—I am still talking to myself as I bow over the toilet—everything is unfolding. All of your resistance is part of that unfolding. So, does this mean all I have to do is allow my life to unfold and quit fighting it? Yes, I think that is what it means. But it doesn't make sense. No, it does not make sense, not even a little sense. I am still, even when I am not aware of being still? Yes, you are still, even when you are not aware of being still. It is only your awareness of Stillness that varies, and even the degree of awareness is Stillness unfolding.

Then why am I fretting about things so much? I have no idea.

Blessings,
    John Conley

P.S. Putting a pencil in a small copper water pipe actually does work, more or less, if you give the pencil a few good whacks with a hammer. You can flush the toilet with a bucket of water until you figure out your next step.

Questioner: Baba Ram Jahn, today I met a young monk who recommended that I fast to accelerate my spiritual growth. Do you think this is necessary, Master?

Baba Ram Jahn: Yes, child, I do. I fast long and hard, nearly everyday. And I am certain this has given me the discipline to pursue spiritual matters. By the way, you are certainly meeting a lot of monks, lately. Aren't they supposed to be meditating and chanting, and doing other monkish things, instead of talking to you?

Questioner: They seem to be very interested in my spiritual progress, especially the young ones. I think it is important for me to let them express their views. This accelerates their spiritual growth through clear thinking and the use of rigorous logic. It is the least I can do for them. And do not try to change the subject, Father. How long do you fast?

Baba Ram Jahn: Usually, my child, I fast to the point of utter starvation, say from after breakfast until lunch. Yes, my fasts are long. For example, today I fasted from after lunch until dinner, except for a small bowl of ice cream. My body felt weak, but I was steadfast in my resolve. Fasts such as these are rigorous and should not be undertaken by novices.

Questioner: Master, you are so silly! I am serious.

Baba Ram Jahn: And so am I, daughter. I hear the call of cookies and milk calling to me from Stillness.

November 20

Dear Friends,

    Do not carry your anger into your sleep tonight, for your life is short, and your time to both seek and give forgiveness is now. When all your books have been set aside, when all your philosophies bring no comfort, when even enlightenment is nothing but a wasted word, then what will be left is who you love and who loves you.

    Little else will matter when your end comes, and your end can and will come, the only mystery is when. Therefore, do not let your anger linger. Do not let fear sway you. Go now and seek forgiveness. For as Christ said, "Ask and it shall be given." All of your riches will mean nothing when your end comes. Were you famous? That will not matter when your end comes. Were you enlightened? Did you have heavenly visions? Did you have deep insights? Those will pass. What will matter is this. The smile on your daughter's face. The laugh in your beloved's voice. The skip in your son's step. The awkward hug of a good friend.

    And this will matter too. The hurt look on your daughter's face. The cry of pain in your beloved's voice. The shuffle of your son's step. The turned shoulder of a good friend. These things will matter. These things will matter and only these things.

    Do you find yourself unable to forgive? Were you abused? Were you beaten? Were you misunderstood and deserted? Did you fight in a war and see and do things no one should ever do and see? Is it impossible to forgive? No. Forgiveness is a letting go, only that and nothing more. And letting go is a simple journey to the heart.

Letters to My Friends

Forgiveness is taking your hurt and regret into Stillness and holding it there until it dissolves.

This is what I shared with a friend recently. It was my poor attempt to share my entry into forgiveness, into courage. The breath is the broad gateway to Stillness. The breath takes us into the energy and the energy is the edge of Stillness, and the Stillness is God.

As we breathe in, we can feel the energy rising from our bellies up through our hearts and our throats and into our eyes. And as we breathe out, we can feel the energy healing every fiber of our being as it flows through us. Pain stands no chance against this healing flow of Stillness. The Stillness is a river. The pain is a rock. Look at the rock with compassion. Look at the rock without judgment. Feel the rock. Is it in your belly, your chest? Your throat? Breathe and feel the Stillness flow around the rock. Keep breathing. Put your awareness on the Stillness under the breath. Soon the rock, whether it is a feeling or thought, young or old, deep or shallow, will dissolve. It will dissolve. And when it does, you will find peace.

New rocks may appear. Or old ones you thought long gone may rise again. But they cannot stand against the wash of Stillness. Stillness washes away all hurt, all hate, and leaves love in its place. Stillness leaves joy.

Does this sound too simple to work? Perhaps so, but has your endless agonizing released you from your pain? Has thinking and thinking and thinking about a problem released you from its grip? It never has me. But holding my pain in Stillness works, and for that I am grateful.

For I know that my end is near, if not today, then tomorrow or the next day, or twenty years from now. But my end is near. And I have no time for hate, for fear, for anger. I have no time for regret. I will seek forgiveness, both from myself and from others. I will give forgiveness, both to myself and to others. When I see my son, I want to see a big smile. When I see my daughters, I want to see shining eyes. When I see my beloved, I want to see laughter on her face. I want my friends to welcome me. For me, this is enough. This is enlightenment. This is awakening.

I am not talking here about clinging to others, of demanding that others heal me. I cannot control a single event in the world. To think otherwise is an illusion. But I can act passionately. I can forgive passionately. I can embrace those I love passionately. And I can leave the results of my actions to something that is both greater and smaller than myself.

And above all, I can enter into Stillness passionately. To enter into a lifetime of Stillness, I must enter into a year of Stillness. And to enter into a year of Stillness, I must enter into a month of Stillness. And to enter into a month of Stillness, I must enter into a day of Stillness, and to enter into a day of Stillness I must enter into an hour of Stillness, and then a minute and then a second. And then, finally, to have a lifetime of Stillness, I must be still this moment, for in truth, that is all there is.

So now, take a breath. Your breath is but the manifestation of something so vast that we cannot ever describe it adequately, but we can enter into it with passion. So breathe now and live.

Blessings,
    John Conley

Letters to My Friends

Questioner: Tell me, Father, who are you?

Baba Ram Jahn: I used to believe that I was the imaginary character of a man named John. And then I thought he was an imaginary character of mine.

Questioner: And what do you think now, Father?

Baba Ram Jahn: I think we are imaginary characters of each other, and neither of us exist!

Questioner: Do you know what I think, Father?

Baba Ram Jahn: No, daughter, but I suspect you will tell me.

Questioner: I think you are both characters. That is what I think.

November 27

Dear Friends,

When I was a young boy, I threw the shot put. I weighed 140 pounds, at the most. Despite my best efforts, I could never throw the shot put as far as boys who were bigger and stronger than I was.

I do not think I won even a single meet. You see, I did not know how much size mattered, how much fate mattered, or karma. I thought if I gripped the cold iron ball fiercely and planted my feet in the short green grass firmly, and scowled into the distance, that I would win every meet. Only it never worked that way. No matter how determined I was, no matter how much I believed in myself, I still lost. Some 200-pound brute, who worked half as hard as I did, would toss the shot put and win.

Of course, being young, and being determined to win, I did what many young men do. I blamed myself. It was my fault that I lost. There must have been something I could have done. I should have tried harder, worked longer. It never occurred to me that life sometimes was simply the way it was, that sometimes I needed to accept things the way they were.

Later on, in my late teens, I saw my mother blame herself for losing a much bigger contest. She had breast cancer. Over the course of years, it turned into lung cancer, and liver cancer, then brain cancer, and eventually death. And she blamed herself. She believed that if she had faith, God would heal her. And since God did not heal her, she did not have faith and it was her fault.

And there were many faith healers in those days who, when their prayers and supplications failed, were only too eager to agree with her. It was her fault. If she had faith, she would be healed. Of course, the Reverend Daniel never said that, not once. He had something else to say. More about that later.

And now, these many years later I am flirting with the blame again. I have bladder cancer. It's still in the early stages. This month I go in for my second surgery. So, it is not as early as I would like! I get tired, and I'm in pain, not a lot of pain, but more than I would like, which, of course, is none.

I read recently a book by a famous spiritual writer who said that illness is always, always the result of unconscious guilt, which results in negative belief systems, which in turn manifest negative thoughts.

I thought, "Oh great! Not only do I have cancer, but I don't have the right beliefs either. And it's all my fault."

The views of this writer are the same as my mother's Christian fundamentalist views. Both claim that illness comes about because of a lack in the individual. My mother believed she could not be healed because she lacked faith. This writer—and many believe as he does—believes that illness is a result of unconscious guilt. This sounds very much like the same gift wrapped in different paper.

I think this is a big universe, not given to simplistic answers. I think my mother was a loving woman who loved God. She had faith. She had the faith to raise two boys and a girl, a dog, a chicken, a cow, and several cats while she battled cancer year after year. She had the faith to love my father and comfort him, even on her deathbed. She had the faith to inspire the doctors and nurses she met. She had the faith to teach me the meaning of courage, not the kind that makes it into newspapers, but the kind that just keeps plugging away, no matter what the odds. She had the faith to love her violets and her roses until her dying day. And she had the faith to plant herself in my heart these many years later.

So, now, here I am with cancer. Do I need more faith? Absolutely, we all need more faith. Do I harbor unconscious guilt? I am sure I do. Do I think negative thoughts? Of course, I hold them everyday. Is the cancer my fault? No, I do not think so, not unless that which I call God is an evil prankster. Can my cancer be healed through positive thinking, or through the relinquishment of unconscious guilt, or through the balancing of my energy system? Perhaps. But, I think these views are half-truths, ones responsible for causing much guilt among those who have an illness.

This is what I do believe. Thinking that arises from Stillness has a powerful influence on my whole life. Stillness is my answer, and therefore I practice Stillness. Sometimes it is easier than at other times. But I have learned not to judge my practice. I simply rest in the Stillness, and I send light to my body which has served me for many years. I thank it for its service. I send love to the cancer too. And I gently ask it to go somewhere else. Perhaps it could go into a dirt clod! Or it could visit the sun. The cancer is not evil. It has no intention of harming me.

Now, the Stillness influences my thoughts and feelings. The more I practice Stillness, moment by moment, the more at peace I feel. And, as a result, my thoughts and feelings tend to be positive with no effort on my part.

When I am tired, which seems to be more and more often, I accept it. I try to rest. I accept that the cancer is. I do not accept that I will have it forever. I accept my own death, but I do not accept that I will die of this cancer. But if I do, so be it. There are many things I do not understand in this life. Illness is one of them. I do know everyone dies and to fight death and fear death is a waste.

And I know that always there is Stillness, and I keep returning to it. And there I find a peace that passes my understanding. If there is healing to be found, it is there in Stillness, beyond all my beliefs.

You might be curious about what Reverend Daniel said to my mother. Dan was a Mennonite minister in a little town in Oregon, where I grew up. He had curly brown hair and a gentle smile. Many was the night he played chess with me when I know he had other things to do. I think he was a saint. He said this, "Helen, I do not understand why things happen the way they do. There's so much I do not understand. But I know this, Helen. God loves you."

And so God does. By whatever name we utter, God loves us.

Blessings,
    John Conley

Baba Ram Jahn: Child, over the years we have spoken many times of the Tao. Tell me what you know of the Tao.

Questioner: That, Master, is easy. The dowel cannot be understood or named. But we can see it in the bathroom where it is a part of the towel rack. Indeed, Baba Ram Jahn, without the dowel, there would be no rack.

Baba Ram Jahn: No, daughter, I said the Tao. I am speaking of the ancient Chinese philosophy that speaks of the flow of all things.

Questioner: But of course, Master, when the water flows, the dowel is always ready with a towel. Therefore, Master, without a dowel, there would be no towel, and therefore no flow. And in this sense, all things flow together from the dowel.

Baba Ram Jahn: Child, you remind me of me, more and more everyday.

Questioner: It is the dowel, Baba Ram. All things flow from the dowel.

December 4

Dear Friends,

Who am I that I should pretend to know anything? I am nobody and I know nothing. I believe nothing. I have no desire to believe anything. Beliefs confuse me. I have nothing to give, not of myself. Yet, when I turn inward and go beyond the words, I find God, and then I have God, the most precious gift, to give.

My experience of God is Stillness. I have been very good at Stillness. My thoughts float on a river of Stillness. Outward reality often appears as a land of shadows, a land of dreams where the inhabitants are but ghosts. I crave being alone. I shun people. And in the secret pride of my heart, a little voice says, "See me. I am holy."

I laugh at the voice. It's only my little brother, what others call my ego. I laugh at him. Tease him. Sometimes he pouts. But he is with me always, commenting on my experience, judging God, and generally getting in trouble. My little brother is sweet. He wants girls to admire him. He wants the men to envy him. He wants to be recognized and loved. He wants what we all want. He is my inner human.

But I have another voice too. This one I call my soul. He cares for me. Reminds me to enter into Stillness. He gently chides little brother when necessary. I do not think of this voice as my ego. He is truly saintly. He is my connection to the divine.

And then beyond these two voices, there is an awareness that seems endless. This I think of as the edge of God. My own little corner of God. We, the little brother, the soul, and the corner of

God are usually a happy family, but only when we love each other. Whenever we decide to hate our little brother or chastise him too harshly, trouble and pain arise. My little brother has had a hard life. He needs to be loved. Perhaps someday he will disappear into the totality that is God. But on this day, he needs to be loved.

If he has a greedy thought, he needs to be loved. If he has a lustful thought, he needs to be loved. If he feels left out, unrecognized, and jealous, he needs to be loved. That is my job, me the soul, to love him until he sleeps, to comfort him when he is in pain. I feel so sorry for those who do not love their little brothers and sisters. What pain they must endure! How long will they hate themselves, war with themselves, before they learn about love?

I will tell you something. If you hate your ego, your little brother or sister, you hate something God created. You hate something God loves. And let me tell you something else. Until you learn to love your little brother or your little sister, you will never love anybody else. You will never connect with them. How could you, for what you carry in your heart is anger and self-judgment.

So, if you want to love another, pat your little brother on the head. Give your little sister a hug. Listen to their wisdom. Their wisdom is of the earth. Listen to their wisdom and love them. Laugh with them and occasionally at them. In doing so you will discover love.

And once you find love, that aching loneliness we all carry will begin to lessen. Love is the only antidote for loneliness. If we were not men and women, Stillness alone would be enough. It would fill us up and we would have no lack. But we are men and women. We need each other, and it is only love that will fill us up. I am speaking of a love that flows from the divine. In truth love and Stillness are one essence. It is only our experience that differs. When I focus my awareness inwardly, I experience Stillness. When I focus my awareness outwardly, on you, I experience love.

What is this love? Perhaps we should first ask what it is not. It is not hateful. It is not jealous. It does not demand. It does not cling. It does no harm. It does not seek its own gain only. It does not manipulate.

And what is love? It is gentle. It asks for nothing in return except to experience itself in the other. It laughs. It teases. And yes, sometimes, it falls madly passionately in love. It flows gently from God. It is very human. It is where we meet God in the face of the other.

Do you want to experience divine love now? Good. Here is a simple recipe. Think of someone you love. See their face. See their lips. See the laughter and joy in their eyes. Now breathe them into your heart. Feel their warm Stillness there in your heart. You are now in heaven. Keep breathing. Keep loving. Say hello to God in the face of this beloved. Repeat as needed.

Now, here is the most wonderful secret in the universe. As you give love, you receive it. It is so very, very simple. Do you want to swim in love? Then give love. Do you want to be hugged, to be kissed? Then give love. Do you want the aching loneliness to cease, to flee like the Philistines before Israel? Then give love. Love with all your heart. Love knowing your love will fail, that your love will not always be pure. Love knowing that you are human and therefore fallible and love all the more for that knowledge. For it is your devotion to love, not the perfection of your love, that will move God to tears. It is so very simple.

Blessings,
    John Conley

John C. Conley

Questioner: Baba Ram Jahn, your brother gave me a koan today.

Baba Ram Jahn: What is it, dear heart?

Questioner: If your wife says you're wrong, and you're not there to hear her, are you still wrong?

Baba Ram Jahn: And what do you think, daughter? This is a most delightful koan.

Questioner: I think, Father, if mother says you are wrong, you better be wrong, or it will not be delightful for long!

December 11

Dear Friends,

Who are you my friends? You gaze at me with liquid eyes full of joy. Please, tell me who you are that I may know you. Your lips gently smile. Who are you with your joyful laughter? Who are you?

Tell me who you are that I may know you. Are you merely faces, passing through on your way to eternity? Am I to know you but for a while and then no more? No, that can not be. Then tell me, who are you? What is that I hear? You are God?

Yes, of course, you are God. How could I have been so blind? Please forgive me that I have not recognized you and bade you welcome. Please forgive me any harm I may have caused you. Please forgive me for not seeing this sooner. I was so blind, surrounded by God, yet in a cloud of unknowing.

But in you now I see joy and laughter, love and life. I see all that makes life worth living. I see God in you. And if I should ever forget, please remind me. Remind me with a gentle smile. A kind laugh. A silly joke. Remind me with a soothing touch. Hug me. Share with me who you are. Share with me, my friends, Share with me who you are.

And forgive me my future transgressions. There will be times when I love too much, too soon. Carry me with you. And there will be times I love too little, too late. Again, carry me with you. There will be days when I long for you, ache for you; and there will be days when I pull back, when I hide. Carry me with you.

And if you forget who you are, I will remind you. And dear God, please see yourself in us. Fill our loneliness with your love, for our loneliness is deep and can only be filled by you. Yes, we will remind each other who we are. And we will fill each other up. We will be as jasmine to each other, allowing the fragrance of our souls to awaken each other.

And together, dear hearts, all of us together, simply by being who we are, we will change the world.

Blessings,

John Conley

Questioner: Baba Ram Jahn, I think I want to be a writer when I grow up. What do you suggest?

Baba Ram Jahn: Sweet daughter of my heart, this is what I would tell you. Use commas, colons, and semi-colons liberally. Write long sentences and then short sentences. Learn a few quotes, from Nietzsche and Fukow, from Jung and Freud, from Plato and Aristotle; and, if you cannot find a quote you like, make it up. And then learn a few learned words, such as epistemological, ontology, theology, proctology, and urology. Sprinkle these words judiciously in both your conversation and writing and you will be a writer.

Questioner: But Father, don't I need something wise to say?

Baba Ram Jahn: Of course not, my flower, of course not. If that were the case, there would be only a few thousand books. I would certainly be out of business, for I am not wise.

Questioner: Oh, but Father, you are wise, for is not the one who acknowledges ignorance the one who is wise?

Winter

December 18

Dear Friends,

    I ran up to her and knelt down in front of her, for she was sitting in the lotus position. I threw my arms around her and hugged her hard. "I love you," I gushed into her ear. She laughed and said, "I love you too." And she hugged me until my heart melted. And so I learned about receiving love.

    And so begins my story about Aurora. When, not long ago, I was in the enchanted land of Maui to listen to many wonderful teachers, my sangha brothers and sisters encouraged me to go to yoga class. I swallowed my pride and went to the class. I am about as flexible as a fence post. And, even though I practice Stillness, even though I have meditated for many years, and even though I strive for wisdom and knowledge, I nevertheless am a man, and I do not like to look ridiculous.

    Aurora, our yoga teacher, radiated gentleness. She made me feel like a great yogi. My heart felt drawn to her. My dear Joan taught first grade for many years. Often I have seen little children run up to her, grab her leg, and yell, "I love you." That is how I felt with Aurora, like a little boy, only I did not grab her leg.

    Now, that night, I saw Aurora again. We were both listening to a wonderful kirtan wala chant the names of God. She came up to me. Hugged me, and with a kind laugh, said, "Do you still love me?" And I said, "More than ever." And so I learned even more about receiving love. I am not sure yet what I learned. It may take years. But I will try to explain it.

    Aurora allows this energy that I am calling love to flow through her. She is gentle beyond words. Her presence caressed my heart as though with a soft stirring of wind. I am sure that all of us in her yoga class fell madly in love with her. Yes, this energy of love flowed through her. And she absorbed our love with grace and humor. Somehow, someway, Aurora had become so rooted in Presence that our love did not frighten her. No, indeed not. She took her meals with us. She attended satsang with us. She joined us as we chanted. She became a member of our impromptu sangha. She hugged us and petted us and loved us. And I think in doing so, we came to love ourselves a little bit more. And we came to love each other a little bit more.

I teased my friend Rajneesh that he was the teacher's pet. He looked stunned and said, "No, you're the teacher's pet." And it dawned on me that her love made us all feel like the teacher's pet.

I adored Aurora and I still do. And I want to learn from her. So I ask myself, "How did she make us all feel so special?" And I answer myself that it was not so much what she did, although that was wonderful, it was what she was. She was love. She had somehow tapped into that flow of love until the flow became her.

And that is what I want to do. I want to tap into that flow. Or do I? When I tap into that flow, I do not know myself. I say things in a language foreign to me; things like, *Dear One*, and *Sweetheart*, and *Dear Heart*! I tell people I love them. I hug people. Sometimes I hug them until I feel their hearts melt. I worship my friends. I see God in them. And I get all soft inside. This is truly terrible. I deserve your pity. I really do.

As I told one friend, "I know what it is to be tough." Yes, indeed, I was a soldier and a commercial fisherman. I worked with crazy loggers. I took risks for the fun of it. I have faced death many times and laughed at it. Well, maybe I chuckled. Would you believe I gave a smile, a little one? Anyway, I did all those things, and now here I am, years later, saying, "I adore you."

I cannot blame this transition totally on Aurora. I cannot take her to love court, because I must admit, that the first day I stepped into the flow of Stillness, I also stepped into the flow of love. Only I did not know it!

It is hard for me to explain. I thought I could stay in Stillness forever, safe from being misunderstood, safe from rejection, safe from being hurt by you. For me, Stillness was of the mind, and love was of the heart. In Stillness, I felt a compassion. In love, I felt vulnerable. In love, I could be hurt.

I thought to protect myself in Stillness. But it did not work that way. No, it did not. My heart got opened through the back door. And now it will not shut. Yikes! What am I going to do? What am I supposed to do? How am I supposed to act? It was so much easier when I was a kid. I would get mad and punch somebody. It was so simple. Now, I rarely get mad. I am always falling in love. And I want to hug people. Oh my God!

So, here is my suggestion. Never go into Stillness. Strange things happen there, things you might not like. Who knows, you too might end up like Aurora, warm, gentle, funny, and loving. Wait! I hear a little voice whispering to me. It's saying, "Sorry, John, it's too late. They're already that way!" Well folks, I'm sorry. I'm not saying this whispering voice is from God. It's probably just my imagination. But you never know.

Too bad, dear ones, you have been drafted into the army of love. I suggest you go see Aurora for basic training.

I adore you reluctantly,
    John Conley

P.S. Aurora, I think I really was your favorite!

Letters to My Friends

Questioner: Master, what are the main differences in Judaism, Christianity, and Islam.

Baba Ram Jahn: Let me think for a moment. They all revere Abraham as their spiritual father. They all believe in one God, the same God, by the way. They all teach love, compassion, and forgiveness. And many, many good and wonderful people abide by all three faiths. There, I think that summarizes it well enough.

Questioner: But, Father, those are not differences! They all believe in the same fundamental truths.

Baba Ram Jahn: Holy mackerel! Questioner, do you think anyone else noticed this? Should we tell them?

Questioner: Yes, Baba, let's tell anyone who will listen!

December 25

Dear Friends,

Once, not so long ago, a young woman—call her Traveler—told me she had a dream, or perhaps it was a vision. I do not remember. And in that dream the two of us lived in a Tibetan monastery. She was a monk and I was the lama. After she told me about the dream, we chatted about reincarnation, but inwardly I laughed that anyone would think that I had once led a Tibetan monastery. How could anyone believe that about me?

Later that night I told my wife, Joan, about the dream Traveler had. And I said, "I sure have come down in the world. I must have done something awful to end up in this life." I hurt Joan's feelings. She came close to tears. I apologized. I asked for forgiveness and I meant it sincerely, but it took me many, many months, in truth until tonight, for me to realize what I had done.

Here is what I had done. I had rejected Traveler, for I did not deem myself worthy to be a spiritual guide, even though her heart told her I had been. I had rejected Joan by saying that this life we have together was not as important as the life of a Tibetan lama. I had rejected myself for denying the impact for good I have on others in this life. But, above all, I had rejected Spirit by not seeing that my life is exactly as it should be.

Always, no matter where I am, I am one breath away from that which I seek, always one breath away. I am one loving gaze from that which I seek. Never more. When I smell the blossoms of the apple tree, I am as close to God as is the blossom to the branch. When I taste the dew on a wild strawberry on a clear mountain morning, I am as close to God as I will ever be.

Letters to My Friends

To say otherwise is to reject God. This is the life I was given. This is the life I need. To say that the greatest teachers of all time—Abraham, Moses, David, Jesus, Mohammed, Krishna, Ram, Buddha, and Lao Tse—were any closer to God than I am now is simply wrong. I will never be closer. I will never be further away. It is only my heart that tells me I am distant. It is only my mind that keeps me distant.

I cannot be any closer than I am now. No other life, no matter how exulted, will bring me closer. Should I win acclaim and be acknowledged as a great spiritual teacher, I will be no closer. With all my many flaws, I am close to God. Were all my flaws removed, I would be no closer. For God knows that all true goodness arises from the Stillness within my heart. I could do great works and be no closer to God. I could feed the poor and be no closer to God. I could heal the sick and be no closer to God.

I am one, just one, embrace away from God. As I embrace you, so I embrace God. As I behold the beauty in your face, so I behold the beauty in the face of God. As I profess my love to you, so I profess my love to God. If I say I love God, and do not love you, then I am a liar.

My relationship with the divine is not about the path I follow, the meditative practices I follow. It is not about my thoughts or the absence of my thoughts. It is not about my feelings. My relationship is simply there, and already complete. God surrounds me. I need do nothing except give thanks.

And if this is true of me, is it not also true of you? When you see me, do you see God? When you embrace me, do you embrace God? When you smile at me and say "I love you," do you not also say this to God? When you ask me to see God in myself, are you not then God yourself? Do you not then see God in yourself?

In saying yes to God in each other, we will save the world from the darkness that enfolds it. In saying yes to each other, we will save each other from the darkness that enfolds us. We will save each other from not knowing we are God. And in so doing we will save God. How else can it be?

So be still. Love. Laugh. Enjoy. Cry. Be sad. Be hurt. Feel confused. Give a hug. Fall madly in love. Be rejected. Be misunderstood. Fail and fail grandly. Be intense. Say silly things. Make a fool of yourself for love. And know that in the end, only love will last, for only love is eternal.

Blessings,
John Conley

Questioner: Baba Ram Jahn, when did you become interested in God?

Baba Ram Jahn: Child, I cannot remember ever not being interested in God. My earliest memories are of God.

Questioner: That sounds so boring! There is so much more to life than God!

Baba Ram Jahn: No, daughter. I would go to church and get saved. I got saved so many times! I lost count. All the grown ups cried and said how cute I was. They patted me on the head. I loved getting saved! It was great fun.

Questioner: I think I am going to pray for you, Father. God needs to save you from being saved!

January 1

Dear Friends,

The ghosts [of our past] are our angels given a different name.

—Shivani

My sorrow points me to Stillness; and sorrow, throughout my life, has been my companion, my one constant companion. I was born with a burden of sorrow. It weighed me down. I felt as though I were wading uphill in the mud and carrying the burden of the whole world on my shoulders.

Even as a young boy, where others laughed and played, I sat silently and watched as despair wracked my heart. I knew something was wrong, desperately wrong. All the laughter in the world could not hide the ocean of suffering I saw in both myself and others. And I knew too that it was my job to heal it. So, of course, I ran. As I grew into a man, I threw myself with abandon into every form of escape. But no matter how far I ran, I knew I had a calling. I had to heal the sorrow. But how was I to do that?

Was I supposed to stand on street corners and shout the truth? What truth? There was no truth other than the world was stuck in a vast sea of despair. That was the only truth I saw. I spent many years reading about every religion in the world, both minor and major. And yet I did not believe a single one of them pointed to the truth, let alone grabbed the truth.

Was I supposed to believe that a loving God would sacrifice his own son? Is God then worse than the most hideous criminal? What would you say if your neighbor nailed his son to the cross?

Was I supposed to believe that God loved the Hebrews but hated the Egyptians? The soldiers that drowned in the Red Sea, did they not have mothers and fathers, brothers and sisters, sons and daughters? Did God hate them so much that he had to destroy them? Could he not simply have built a wall?

And did I have to believe that those who did not believe in Allah, those who did not follow the writings of Mohammed, would spend eternity in hell? Is that what a loving God does?

Or perhaps I could believe that my own nature had to be overcome. My every desire, hope, and dream, that which made me human, stood between me and the infinite. I had, in essence, to annihilate myself to be united with the universe. There would be nothing of me left. So why, I wondered, create me in the first place?

Everything I read seemed silly. If God were this ignorant, this vicious, this horrible, I wanted nothing to do with him. Yet, I continued to search, for my sorrow would not give me any respite. I felt I had two choices, either die or find God. So, I died, again and again and again. I repeatedly destroyed everything I loved. I hurt everyone I loved. And I came to despise myself. I loathed myself with an unfaltering passion.

Now, I will tell you something. I have not changed one bit since those days, not one little bit. I still think nearly everything I hear about God is silly. Please forgive me, but I do. But now there is a difference. I am like a man who wandered in the desert for years searching for water. I would find water, but instead of drinking it, I would say, "I do not understand this water. And I do not understand this desert." And away I would go again, wandering in the desert, looking for water.

But one day, I came upon the water a final time. Despair had seized me, had robbed me of all strength, and I fell into the water. It flowed over me, it soothed my burnt body and quenched my desperate thirst. And slowly, slowly, the gentle flow of water washed the desert sand from my eyes. And I finally understood. And this is what I understood.

I will never understand, never. I will never know why children suffer. But the water soothes me. I will never understand the source of my own sorrow. But the water soothes me. I will never even know God. But the water soothes me.

This water is Stillness, joy, love. I do not know what to call it. I only know I want to stay in it, for the desert of my sorrow is yet there, stretching on forever, stretching on beyond my own comprehension.

So then, do I have a calling? Perhaps I do. Yes, perhaps I do. But I do not have any answers. My mind goes blank when anyone engages me in learned discussions. I truly do not know what to say. So, if I do not have answers, what is my calling?

It is this. When I was a boy, I lived near one of the most beautiful rivers in the world, the Santiam. The Santiam was my backyard. Its fresh, cool, clear waters brought joy into my life. I skipped rocks there. I built rafts there. I swam there and dived. I played there and laughed with my friends. But I understand only one thing about it. I loved it. And now I am in a different river, the river of Stillness. And my calling is to speak of this river. Yes, this is my calling. And I am calling to anyone who will listen. "Let's swim and have fun. Let's laugh and dive. Let's build rafts. There's room for everyone here in this river. The shore never gets crowded and the water is always clear." So, that is my calling and that is all I know. Are you listening? I hope so, for in truth, it is not I who am calling. It is our sorrow that is calling, for it is our sorrow that blesses us and calls us into Stillness.

Blessings,
    John Conley

Baba Ram Jahn: Tell me, my daughter, what is your favorite koan?

Questioner: I think, Father, my favorite cone is the one from the Douglas fir, for this cone has neither pitch nor sap on it. Whereas, as I am sure you know, a pinecone nearly always has both pitch and sap.

Baba Ram Jahn: No, no, daughter, I said koan, as in . . .

Questioner: Then why didn't you say so, Master? I like vanilla cones best, for they are simple, pure, and elegant, without adornment or pretense. What is your favorite cone, Father?

Baba Ram Jahn: If there is no one to understand it, does the koan exist?

Questioner: Ah, but Father, there is no need to understand. We must only taste!

January 8

Dear Friends,

    I do not always know who I am, but I know who I am not. I am not that hateful inner voice whose only goal is, it sometimes seems, to destroy me. In the book *Harry Potter and the Prisoner of Azkaban*, author J. K. Rowling sets dementors loose on Harry Potter. These creatures attempt to suck all the happy memories from poor Harry and leave nothing but despair. My hateful inner voice is a dementor.

    My dementor is what Eckhart Tolle calls a pain body, not just a little pain body but a huge, menacing one who tries to stop my spiritual growth by spewing hate.

    Does this shock you? Am I being too honest? Then look within yourself with unclouded sight and courage, and look at your own dementor. Yours may be stronger than mine, or weaker. But it is there. And it will keep you from knowing peace unless you confront it.

    What is the origin of this inner hate? I do not know. I imagine it is what many of us call our ego. It is perhaps a part of our collective unconscious. Or more likely, it is a survival mechanism, one coded into our genes, but one that has gone awry, one that has gone horribly wrong and long ago ceased to be helpful.

    Eckhart Tolle likes to talk about our story, and how we live in our story. He uses this word story in a very specific way. For example, if I stub my toe on a doorjamb, the fact is that I hit my toe. It hurts. And that is all there is to it. Ah, but here is my story, "You are so clumsy," my inner destroyer says. "You can't do anything right. What a fool. And you're not very spiritual, are you? Or you wouldn't be thinking this way. Spiritual people accept things calmly. Spiritual people would never manifest this kind of accident."

Yes, my inner destroyer is nasty, nasty, nasty. I do not like him. I want to avoid him. I want to stuff him into a dark corner of my mind until he chokes on his own words and cannot be heard. I hate him and he hates me. He hates everything.

I want to destroy him. But wait. I have tried that, and I have learned a very hard lesson. My inner destroyer feeds off of my resistance. My anger makes him grow and gives him strength. He feeds like a hyena at the carcass of my resistance. So what am I to do? I could spend years and years trying to understand why I think the way I do. I could blame my mother and father, and their mothers and fathers, and their mothers and fathers. Eventually, if I keep blaming long enough, I end up blaming God. Who else is there to blame?

But blaming others will not rid me of my dementor. Nor, will understanding my history rid me of my dementor. I could analyze my personal psychology from here to eternity and come no closer to joy. So what am I to do?

Christ said to love my enemies. So, if I am my own enemy, I must love myself. I must embrace that part of myself I most loathe. I must love the part of me that I hate. There is no other way to peace. But how do I embrace that which I loathe? If understanding myself is not the key then what is?

Stillness, of course, and then more Stillness, and then yet more Stillness. But remember, Stillness is just one aspect of Source. It is my favorite aspect, but there are others—love, naturally, and joy and courage. The Source of all things is that which we need in the moment.

So, where does this leave us? I can only tell of my own experience. Recently, for example, I think I upset a friend, someone very

Letters to My Friends

dear to me. This is serious to me, because I value my friends. My inner destroyer was only too glad to help. "You are an idiot," he said. "You should never leave the house. Every time you open your mouth, you say something stupid." I instantly began to resist. "No, that's not true. Everyone makes mistakes." And the battle raged. Me against me, with me losing.

Suddenly, I noticed the Stillness at the center of my being. With each breath I took, I felt a gentle joy throughout my entire body. As I focused on this Stillness, my joy grew stronger until it suffused me from head to toe. And then I invited my inner destroyer in, and I let him rant and rave. I felt his pain and fear. I felt his rage. And I held him in Stillness. And the noise lessened until all I heard was a despairing cry, "All I want to do is help." Soon all that was left was the Stillness, the love, the joy of that unnamable Source.

And, my friends, that leaves us with a path to follow, one which we all started long ago. We must find, for our very lives depend on it, the Stillness within each of us. We must find our Source. So, sleep well. The morning comes soon and God awaits us on our path. And we shall each learn, yet again, as Harry Potter did, that hate is no match for joy.

Blessings,
    John Conley

Questioner: Master, do you believe in magic?

Baba Ram Jahn: Yes, child, I do.

Questioner: Do you believe in spells and potions and flying brooms? I would love to be in a Quiddich match with Harry Potter.

Baba Ram Jahn: I believe in the magic of joy that resides in my heart. It is more potent than any spell. I would not change it for any other power. And I believe also in the magic of love.

Questioner: That is wonderful, Master. But think of soaring through the sky on a magical broom. Think how wonderful that would be! Is not the joy of dreams the same as the joy of God?

Baba Ram Jahn: Yes, child, I think it is. Joy is joy. We could try hang gliding. That would be a little like Quiddich!

Questioner: I think, Father, I will settle for make believe! Joy is joy.

January 15

Dear Friends,

    I believe that each of us must have the courage to have a religion of one. My beliefs pertain to me and only to me and only for this moment. I make absolutely no effort to be consistent. I make no effort to build from what I have said before. Indeed, I realize I have contradicted myself again and again. I am pleased with my contradictions, immensely pleased.

    And why am I pleased? It is because I never want to know God in some sort of final way. I never want to be so certain of myself that I become dogmatic, that I think I know the way. There is no one way. And it is ridiculous to think so. We live in an infinite universe, yet we are often like musicians who play in one key and use one scale and we refuse to admit there are other keys. We demand that everyone play in this key and only this key. We want to put God in a musical box that plays only one tune!

    Moses put the wild God, the unconfined God, of Abraham in a box and carried Him around in the desert. The Hebrews proclaimed themselves the chosen people because they carried God in a box. Yet, the Muslims and the Christians believe their way is the right way. They too put God in a box. And the Hindus and the Buddhists know, secretly in their heart of hearts, that their ways are superior. And again, God is in a box.

    We tend to view our spiritual experiences from the viewpoint of our tribe. And the tribe always says, "God loves us best!"

Frequently, the tribe even says, "God abhors sinners." And all who are outside the tribe, by definition, are sinners.

If we are to mature in our spiritual quest, we must have a global view of God. God loves everyone equally; in other words, sinners and saints, the just and the unjust. We are all of us God's chosen people. We are all called to serve God by serving each other.

Yet I think we are also called to have a religion of one. We are called to have an intensely personal God in the sense that our beliefs apply only to us. One day I approach God as an impersonal power of the universe. God is a set of unchanging universal laws. The next day, I pray to God to grant me favors. I would like to go to Hawaii again and see my friends. And I would like to not cry when I see them. I want my daughter to rub my feet. I just rubbed hers. But she has me trained! Is that too much to ask, God?

Another day I experience God as a flow of Stillness. My thoughts drift on the Stillness as leaves on the surface of a creek. Yet another day my consciousness merges with a larger consciousness and I lose all sense of who I am in that larger consciousness. One day I sing to Krishna. The next I sing to Jesus. And the next, I sing about Joshua.

There is no one way. There are many, many, many ways and they are always changing as we learn and grow. We have the wonderful opportunity to be universal spiritual shoppers. We can adopt the void from Buddhism. We can take devotional singing, kirtan, from Hinduism. We can take ecstatic prayer from Judaism. We can take ecstatic dancing from the Sufis. We can take a commitment to service from Christianity. And we can restore our balance with nature through many forms of Shamanism. We have so much from which to chose. Yet we want to put God in that box. We want to cage God so that we are in control.

Who wants a wild God? I do. I want a God about which I

ultimately know nothing. I want a God that is beyond my reasoning, beyond my beliefs, beyond my dogma. I want to have the courage to not know. I want to know God through my experience. I need understand very little to experience God. Actually, the less I understand, the deeper my experience is likely to be.

Have you ever asked yourself why Eckhart Tolle is so hugely popular? There are many wonderful spiritual teachers who have not had nearly the impact of Eckhart Tolle. Why? I think it is because he had the courage to stand alone. He stripped everything down to its essentials. He invited us to have an experience. He took thousands of years of Buddhism and said, "Quit thinking so much. Be still." He took thousands of years of Hinduism and said, "Feel the energy in your hands." He took thousands of years of Christianity and said, "Christ had a simple message. Love your neighbor and love God."

It takes courage to dive into the ocean of God and strip away all the barnacles from the ship of spirit. But that is what Eckhart did. He has been laughed at and scorned, yet his simple message has awakened tens of thousands to their own experience of Being.

All authentic teachers have a simple message; and this, I believe, is that message. "Be still. Love. Be true to your path, and allow others to be true to their path. God will welcome all of us, no matter which path we follow, no matter whose name we utter." If we believe this simple message, we will find ourselves following a wild God, one who refuses to be captured. And we will follow a God who refuses to capture us.

Blessings,
    John Conley

Questioner: I do not know what to do when I grow up.

Baba Ram Jahn: I feel the same way! One day I want to be a surfer, and the next day I want to eat a dozen chocolate chip cookies. Yesterday, I wanted to be a mountain climber. And I have been seriously thinking about being a stunt pilot.

Questioner: But, Father, it takes years to learn to be a stunt pilot! And a surfer who eats too many cookies would make a tasty meal for a shark.

Baba Ram Jahn: God sings in my heart. "Somewhere over the rainbow, bluebirds fly. And the dreams that you dream of really do come true."

Questioner: So, Master, I see what you are saying! Dream wildly! I could be a concert violinist. Or I could be a painter. I could run marathons. I could be a supermodel. I could write great novels. Or be a great spiritual teacher. I could own a horse ranch. I could be a renowned scholar. What remains constant is the song of God in my heart!

Baba Ram Jahn: Yes! Yes, daughter. Growing up too soon, too fast is highly overrated. I am still waiting to grow up! I think I might try growing sideways for a change. Or I might grow down. Or maybe diagonally! Or I could grow in a circle. Or, perhaps, I could learn to grow hair.

January 22

Dear Friends,

For me, both passion and detachment arise from Stillness. I throw myself into the task at hand, whether it is awakening, writing a book, or unclogging a drain. But I divorce myself from the results, which is good, especially when it comes to drains.

This is how I enter into Stillness. And it is from Stillness that I am able to practice passion and detachment. I breathe. I feel my heart beat. I feel the energy of the breath rising from my belly, to my heart, to my chest and throat, and then into my face. I hold the energy in my face for a few long moments. And I breathe out through my heart.

I focus on the felt sense of energy behind the breath. As I do this, my thoughts and feelings tend to slow. Often, to help me focus, I might silently chant *Shanti Om*, with *Shanti* on the in breath and *Om* on the out breath. I may visualize red light coming up from my belly, where it turns into white light in my face.

If the flow of thoughts and feelings will not slow, I might use an affirmation. "Jesus is lord. No harm shall come to me." Or "Krishna is lord. My way is clear." I will say it again and again until all that fills my mind is the affirmation. But I continue to follow the breath and the energy I sense behind it.

When I am still, my breathing tends to slow to three or four breaths each minute. Breathing slowly, breathing with awareness, intent, and deliberation helps me to focus on Stillness, to focus on that which is permanent and unchanging, not on that which is constantly changing.

Always, I am aware of the flow of energy; for this, to me, is the edge of Stillness. Once I am grounded in that flow of energy, my thoughts and feelings arise as they will, with no resistance on my part. They are like autumn leaves in the wind. Occasionally, I will stop thinking altogether. But often my thoughts continue to rise like slow bubbles from the bottom of a marsh. I do not worry about it, one way or the other. The mind thinks. The heart feels. That is what they do. It is the Stillness that counts.

There are times, however, when I attempt to enter into Stillness and a problem keeps intruding. A problem is nothing more than a group of thoughts and feelings strung together. Sometimes it seems as though there is no end to problems. And I feel the urge to understand and solve them. But I could examine all these problems until the day I die and not be one step closer to knowing what to do.

So, what do I do? I simply hold them in this gentle flow of energy as I breathe. Often, a problem will seemingly lodge itself in my heart or throat, or sometimes my belly. I send the energy there. I surround the bodily sensation of constriction with this energy. I breathe into and out of the constriction. I do not try to understand the problem. Insights, solutions, and decisions will come in their own time. I know this may sound so simple that it could not possibly work, but it does. Through this simple technique, I have dissolved problems that have haunted me for my entire life.

Again, it all begins with the breath, the heartbeat, and with becoming aware of the gentle flow of energy. By grace we are awakened. And by grace we awaken ourselves. It is a paradox. The breath. The heart. The flow of Stillness. Passion and detachment. That is all.

Blessings,
    John Conley

Questioner: It has been said, oh Master, that you know all there is to know about chanting. So, please, tell me, what does Hari Krishna mean?

Baba Ram Jahn: Hari Krishna was the older brother of Krishna Das. In ancient India there were no razors, and Hari was exceptionally hairy. All the other gurus used to laugh and call him names, until one day, Krishna Das, whose wife did not like beards, invented the razor blade. Anyway, Krishna Das lent the razor to Hari Krishna, who promptly used it to remove his excess hair. And now these many centuries later, we have the chant, "Hari Krishna," which commemorates that day long ago when Hari Krishna shaved.

Questioner: Yes, but Father, that is not all. I heard that Hari Krishna discovered that he was really a monkey. So he grew all his hair back and joined the monkey god, Hanuman, who helped save the Hari Ram.

Baba Ram Jahn: Daughter! Daughter! Where did you come up with this nonsense? Everybody knows that Hari Krishna joined the British Army and eventually moved to the village of Potter in Scotland, where he opened a barbershop. Hence, the name Hari Potter!

January 29

Dear Friends,

There are days when I am absolutely certain that I know nothing. And on those days, I am probably the closest to the truth. How can I know anything? What I think of as myself is a series of thoughts and feelings that seemingly appear randomly out of nothing and return to nothing. Therefore, I am nothing. If I am nothing, how can I know the answer to any of the important questions life poses? Is God in me? Or am I in God? When I pray, am I praying to myself? If so, am I in trouble?

All this leads me to wonder if our beliefs really make any difference whatsoever in this world. I remember that as a young man, I was convinced that there was one way and only one way to God, and that was through Jesus. Of course, it was not that simple. One had to believe that Jesus died on the cross for our sins and was resurrected on the third day. One further had to believe that Jesus would someday return and reward His people and cast the sinners into everlasting hell. There were many, many things that one had to believe. And in retrospect, not one of those beliefs brought me closer to God.

One day, I was reading in the Old Testament—which book I cannot remember—and God, through one of his prophets, ordered the Israelites to attack a neighboring tribe. And God commanded them to kill every man, woman, child, goat, and sheep in the enemy encampment. I may have gotten the details of the story wrong, but that was the gist of it.

Shortly after reading that passage, I remember listening to a

Christian evangelist telling his congregation that as good Christians we should support the foreign war that was then raging. It was, he said, our Christian duty to stop the spread of evil. Not much, I realized, had changed in the 4000 years between the Hebrew prophet and the Christian evangelist.

I could not believe in a hateful God. I left the religion of my childhood. I still loved Jesus, but I thought most of his followers were misguided. I began to study Hinduism and Buddhism, which opened me up to many, many new paths. And over the years, I realized that in many ways, Hindus and Buddhists were just as much prisoners of their beliefs as the Christians and Hebrews.

It became obvious to me that beliefs separated us not only from God, but also from each other. One only had to read a little history to see that religious zealots had caused many wars and had committed the worst of atrocities in the name of God. War accompanied the spread of Judaism, Christianity, and Islam as a bloody partner. Hindus killed each other. And Buddhists were not immune to war. Still, it was not that I thought organized religions were totally wrong, for I knew good and loving Jews, Christians, Muslims, Hindus, and Buddhists; but it seemed to me—and it still does—that religions set up many roadblocks on the spiritual path, making it almost impossible to find that which we call God.

If I could not find truth in religion, then where was I to find it? In a guru? I could not bring myself to follow a guru. From what I could see, the followers of a guru immediately started a religion and then set themselves against other religions.

No, I could not find truth. And I knew that even if I did, I could not know it was truth. Yet, through all those many years of doubt, something was happening to me. Through failed relationships, through addictions, through illnesses, through nightmarish days and nights of depression, I kept finding little bits of peace. And I found the peace, of all places, within myself. Whenever I could quiet my mind, I felt peaceful, even if only for a few minutes. I tried many forms of meditation in those days, but this was my favorite. I would walk until I hurt, and the pain would quiet my thoughts and I would think only of the pain. And then even the pain would flee, and I would know only peace. To put it another way, in those days walking through the pain was my password to peace.

I first thought of this analogy when, recently, I was getting messages from my phone, and a voice said, "Please enter your password." I went into a daze, which I frequently do, to tell you the truth. Again the voice said, "Please enter your password." I hung up the phone. What was my password? For over thirty years my password had been changing. I had spent much of my adult life looking for the right password, for the magic password. I was like Harry Potter searching for the right incantation. I had tried many forms of religion, and many forms of prayer and meditation. I got lost in the passwords.

And all that time, the passwords did not matter. Like Harry, all I needed was there, waiting quietly within me. I could change the password at will. What mattered was the message at the end of the line. And what was the message? What did I hear?

The message has always been the same for me, always. But for years I ignored it. This is the message. This is what I hear now. I hear love. I can change the password a thousand times a thousand, but the message at the end of the line is eternal. What is my password? It does not matter. Only our experience of the message of love matters, and love has nothing to do with our passwords.

Blessings,
    John Conley

Letters to My Friends

Baba Ram Jahn: Tell me, questioner, what do you know of the Dalai Lama?

Questioner: That is easy, Master. We studied him in school. The Dali Llama is a famous artist who lives in Peru, where he raises llamas and paints. He is so famous that kings and queens, presidents, and prime ministers often go to him to buy paintings. They also buy llamas for long treks through the mountains.

Baba Ram Jahn: No, no, no, daughter. I meant the Dalai Lama who comes from Tibet and is the spiritual head of the Tibetans.

Questioner: Is this a koan, Master? Like one hand clapping? Am I supposed to guess where his body is? That's easy! It's in Peru. You see, the Dali Llama is an abstract artist like Picasso. Time and space mean nothing to him!

Baba Ram Jahn: Ah, perhaps we are talking about the same man! You always amaze me, daughter.

February 5

Dear Friends,

I wonder why I have wasted even one breath on fear when I know my life will end soon. That end may come in a day, a year, or a decade, or even longer, but come it will. Like a relentless fire raging across a dry summer field, my death comes.

So would it not be a blessing, if when we see each other, we smile? Would it not be a blessing if we laughed and shared our joy. Ours is a joy that knows no death, for in this moment we are alive. And if we share our joy, does our blessing spread? Do we not then bless all that is, all that was, and all that will be? Do we not, when we smile, bless the very galaxy in which we live? Do we cause the stars to smile upon us? Do we cause the sun to giggle?

Does Venus sway and Mars dance? Do we cause the moon to smirk as it hides behind a cloud, when we smile? Do we not make the earth give a belly laugh and erupt with geysers and ebullient streams? Do we not cause the very universe to wriggle and flex with power and pleasure?

If, as the ancient ones teach, all is connected to all in a vast web, then when we smile, the very universe smiles. If we smile, we bless both the living and the dead, for we know there is no birth and no death in this universe. The newborn child is as ancient as the most ancient star.

So, again, I wonder, why do I waste even one moment in fear when I know I am eternal? When I breathe, when I breathe slowly and deeply, when I do nothing more than this, I breathe with the earth and all in it. I breathe with the mountains and streams. I breathe with the oceans and the fish in them. I breathe with the sky and with the birds. The clouds become my brothers and sisters. The rain is my mother and the sun my father. When I breathe, I breathe with the planets and the stars and the vast spaces between the planets and the stars. For we are all of us, both big and small, far and near, the breath of God.

I am God breathing me and I am me breathing God. I am both infinitely small and infinitely large. I am confined and I am unconfined. I am the fear and I am the courage that soothes the fear. I am all of this, and I am nothing. I am God, and I am mortal. I wonder much, and I know little.

Often in my life, I go where I am told, and I do what I am told. I fulfill my obligations, and I march to my death. I do what I am told. But in the end, in the final hour, I know that I am the one doing the telling, as well as the one being told. I am the one doing the marching. I am the one doing the dying. For there is the breath and the breath is infinite. Nothing arises by chance, yet all is chaos, for the breath scatters all before it.

And who am I? I am just John, a beloved song of God, and the song comes on the pulsing, beating breath of God. So, when I see you, who do I see? I see a song, a breath, a pulsing, beating breath. I see God when I gaze into your eyes. I see God and seeing God, I know I am never alone. I know I am always loved. I know that I am the hero of this song, and you are the hero of your song, and nothing shall ever defeat or destroy us. I know our songs weave in an infinite, exquisitely beautiful harmony, conducted by God. I know that God is both inside me and outside me. I know that what I believe matters little, for not only am I singing the breath of God, but God is singing me. Each note of my life is from God, the ending note no less than the beginning note.

So, friends, join me while I dance with the moon and kiss the sun. Join me while I laugh at the rivers and chase the high peaks. Join me while I wrestle with our galaxy and tickle the universe. Each breath is forever, and I want to play forever. So join me and play, for in the end, for you, as for me, it is destiny.

Yes, join me in this silliness. Feel the oceans breathing through you. Feel the mountains and the valleys breathing through you. Feel the lakes and streams, and the sky and the clouds breathing through you. And the planets and the stars, feel them breathing through you. Feel the breath of God in your heart. Feel the breath of God giving you life. And now friends, share that breath with me, your friend.

Blessings,
    John Conley

Questioner: Father, I know the answer.

Baba Ram Jahn: The answer to what, child?

Questioner: I know the answer to our favorite koan. "What is the sound of one hand clapping?" The answer is God claps. God moves. God listens. But there is more than that, Father.

Baba Ram Jahn: And what is that?

Questioner: The sound of one hand clapping is a call to God. It says this. "Are you there God? Is anyone listening or am I alone?" And it asks something else, Father.

Baba Ram Jahn: Yes?

Questioner: It is, "Why is this silly old monk waving his hand in the air?"

February 12

Dear Friends,

Whether or not we choose to be, we are all of us teachers. And, in my case, at least, it is fear that keeps me from embracing this. Many years ago, when I started intentionally sharing my spiritual path with others, I promised myself one thing. I would be honest. What a horrible thing to promise myself! My honesty compels me to acknowledge that I am no saint. If anything, I am more of a sinner. If God really does send sinners to hell, I am in trouble. I still get angry and jealous. At times, I am proud and arrogant. I get impatient with people I think are slower than I am. I am stubborn to a fault. I hate to admit I am wrong. I am full of self doubt. I am sometimes indecisive. Or am I?

And worst of all, I have a sense of dread that sometimes clings to me like a fog. And there are days when I cannot find my way out of it. I walk blindly in my dread, fearing that the next step will bring nothing but pain, until I finally remember to be still. In truth, even though I vehemently resist being a teacher, my friends tell me I am. And I suppose that I am, willingly or not, knowingly or not. I am a teacher. But how I resist even yet. Add denial to my list of sins.

So, with all my many faults, what kind of teacher does this make me? Who am I to even pretend that I know anything? How can I possibly think that I have anything to teach? And what do I claim to teach? I teach Stillness. Here is a little story.

In my hometown, a parrot lives in the village hardware store. I love going to that store. It is small and cramped, with many nooks

John C. Conley

and crannies, full of little surprises. I go there frequently. I even make up excuses to go there. Looking at nuts and bolts can be very meditative. I mean who would think nuts and bolts could come in so many shapes and sizes? It is amazing. There are lag bolts and brass screws; wood screws and self tapping screws. I digress!

Now, to the degree that I love that hardware store, I dislike that parrot. His green feathers ruffle as he screeches the same thing over and over again. He always startles me, and all he ever says is, "Hey beautiful! Hey beautiful! Hey beautiful!" He is loud. And he has no idea what he is saying! He screeches at men, women, children, dogs, cats, goldfish, everyone and everything!

Why do I dislike that parrot so much? Obviously, he reminds me of myself. All that ever comes from my beak is "Hey Stillness! Hey Stillness! Hey Stillness!" I say it to anyone who will listen. But if you press me, I cannot tell you what I am saying. I cannot tell you what Stillness is. I can give you a few hints about how to get there. Go left at your breath. Focus on the energy in the road before you. Pay attention to your heart gauge. It's a long trip and you don't want to run out of heart. Don't worry if your mind wanders. Who cares? Just remember to return your attention to the road. What will you find when you get to Stillness? Damned if I know. I only just started the trip myself. But the ride is beautiful; a little bumpy at times, but beautiful.

Sometimes, it seems as though my honesty takes me into a fearful place. And now we are back where we began. We are all teachers. We all have people who trust us and need our message. We must not let fear prevent us from being who we are. Our honesty may lead us to acknowledge our shortcomings, and that is a good thing, unless it takes us into fear. We all have shortcomings. And our fear is founded, in part, on a false view of enlightenment. Enlightenment is a journey with no end through an infinite universe. It is not a point in time or a place in line that we can measure and say, "I have arrived."

We have all of us just begun that journey. The most famous teachers of today are mere feet ahead of us. And some may be behind us. But they have loud voices like that parrot in the hardware store.

Again, we are all of us teachers, without exception. We teach every minute of every day. We must courageously follow our own path, however lonely and frightening that may feel. And then we must be willing to fearlessly, yet gently, share that path. We must not wait for perfection. With all our frailties, I believe we must press onward today. Why? Because the world desperately needs us and we must not succumb to fear. So what is it we will choose? As for myself, I choose Stillness.

Blessings,
    John Conley

John C. Conley

Questioner: Baba, Baba, are you asleep?

Baba Ram Jahn: Yes, child, I am asleep.

Questioner: Then how can you answer me?

Baba Ram Jahn: We gurus are very mystical and powerful. In our sleep we are awake.

Questioner: That explains so much, Baba! If gurus are awake when they are asleep, it follows that they are asleep when they are awake. And that explains why gurus so seldom make sense! Thank you, Baba. Now I understand everything.

Baba Ram Jahn: Yes, daughter, I am very wise. Now can I go back to sleep? We gurus must be ever vigilant.

February 19

Dear Friends,

I am that which I seek. If I seek joy, it is to be found deep within my being. Joy may manifest as a walk in the woods with a friend. Or it may manifest as hugging one of my daughters. It may manifest as reading a good book and gaining new insights. Or perhaps it will manifest as holding hands with a loved one. But the source of joy resides within me.

I am that which I seek. If I seek courage, it is to be found deep within my being. It may manifest as the courage to write these letters and share them. It may manifest as the courage to be honest about my faults. It may manifest as not pretending to be something I am not. It may manifest as speaking up for justice when it would be easier to say nothing. But the source of courage resides within me, always within me.

I am that which I seek. If I seek love, it is to be found deep within my being. Love may manifest as going to work in the morning so that my children can go to college. It may manifest as calling my brother when I am tired and want only to rest. It may manifest in talking to my son and staying calm when I feel irritated. Love may manifest in a smile. It may manifest in encouragement. It may manifest as sacrificing what I want for the welfare of another. But the source of love resides within me.

I am that which I seek. If I seek abundance, it is to be found deep within my being. Abundance may manifest as a clean, beautiful, and loving home for my family. It may manifest as enough money to enjoy a trip to Maui. It may manifest as enough money to pay all the bills. It may manifest as an abundant supply of good food. Like Doritos! But the source of abundance resides within me.

I am that which I seek. If I seek heaven, it is to be found deep within my being. Heaven may manifest as a yearning for itself. Heaven may manifest as courage in the face of death. Heaven may manifest as a desire to dance. Heaven may manifest as a desire to serve others.

I am that which I seek, and what I seek above all is Stillness, for to me Stillness is the fountain from which all else I seek manifests. Stillness is my word for God. And like God, Stillness for me is a mystery, an enigma. Stillness is not quiet. It can be noisy and flamboyant. When I touch Stillness, I am touching nothingness. Yet when Stillness touches me, I feel as though my mother is caressing my cheek.

I will never understand Stillness. Yet that will not keep me from trying! Stillness leads me to embrace this world, like a man embracing his beloved. I do not seek to transcend this world. For if this world is God manifested, why would I reject it? Why would I seek to overcome it? I do not understand.

Nor do I think Stillness requires much from us in the way of ritualistic approaches. I seek simplicity in all things. If I choose to sit when I meditate, I will sit. Stillness does not care what posture I take to meditate. If I choose one mantra over another, Stillness does not care. What is Stillness to be bound by a mantra? The very thought surprises me. Do I need seven chakras with corresponding sounds and colors? No! Do I need fourteen levels of Samadhi? No! Do I need to refrain from work on the Sabbath? No! Do I need to bow when I pray? No! What is Stillness to be bound by these forms? We are the ones who are bound. Why insist on binding that which we call God as well?

And now I have come full circle, for to me Stillness is the experience of joy, courage, love, abundance, and heaven here in this

Letters to My Friends

world today. Stillness resides within us, within the deep spaces of our being. We need only listen and that which is hidden will emerge. Yet Stillness cannot ultimately be understood with our minds. It can only be experienced. Stillness is known by Stillness and Stillness alone. Therefore, this is my message to myself. I am that which I seek.

Blessings,
    John Conley

> Questioner: Baba Ram Jahn, I have been thinking. For every experience there must be an infinite number of explanations for that experience. How can we know which one is the correct interpretation?
>
> Baba Ram Jahn: We cannot, my child.
>
> Questioner: But, Baba, that is awful! How do we know how to live?
>
> Baba Ram Jahn: We cannot, daughter, ever know how to live. But we can choose to follow love. The great Rabbi Hillel once said, "What thou thyself hatest, to no man do." I think we cannot go wrong if we follow the wise Rabbi.
>
> Questioner: Father, that is amazing. Such wisdom. And from a rabbit too! But what about women, Baba? Can we hurt them? Did the Wise Rabbit think about women?
>
> Baba Ram Jahn: Oh, I'm sure he meant women and men. But love gets lost in the translation.

February 26

Dear Friends,

I love to sing kirtan—Hindu devotional songs. Often, I do not even know what the words mean, but when I sing these songs of devotion to Rama and Krishna; and to Shakti and Kali, something strange happens to me. I forget who I think I am. I am no longer John the husband, father, brother, son, and friend I know myself to be. All my history drops away and I become someone else, and that someone else frightens me.

Jaya Bhagavan. Jaya Bhagavan. Jaya. Jaya. Jaya Bhagavan.

That someone else is a little boy. He especially comes out to play when I sing with friends. He behaves in ways not always to my liking. He admires all the men. They are his heroes. He falls in love with all the women. He worships their divine beauty and their gentleness. He wants to hug everyone. He wants everyone to love him. He is, to put it bluntly, not at home in this world. He knows very little about rules, and cares even less.

Hare Rama. Hare Rama. Rama Rama. Hare Hare.

He looks out from my eyes and he sings the names of God with passion. He gets up and dances, not with any skill, but with abandonment. Love pours through him and he gets lost in God. He gets lost in the many faces of God around him. Temporarily they have names like Kendra and Jeff. But really they are God. They gaze at him with blue eyes and brown eyes. They gaze at him with old faces and young faces. And he gets lost. *Jaya Hanuman. Jaya Hanuman. Jaya. Jaya.*

This little boy gets lost, and God reaches out and embraces him. And I think I know why. The part of me that really yearns for the divine is that little boy. He, the innocent one who is lost in this world, is the one who craves God. It is only when I allow myself to be this little boy that I can meld with God. And when I sing to the Gods with my playmates, I allow myself to be that little boy.

He Ma Durga. Ma Durga. Jay Jay Ma.

Oh this is so silly. So funny. I, the John I think of as myself, do not even believe in a personal God. And I certainly do not believe in a God who comes to me when I sing. Yet that is exactly what happens. God comes to me and I get wrapped up in God. And God pours through me until my body feels on fire. I can barely contain myself. I want to throw myself into the arms of all whom I meet and shout, "I love you, God!"

Govinda Hare. Gopala Hare

But if I did that, I would surely get in trouble. The world is not ready for God. Nor is the world ready for us when we get lost in God. Nor, are we always ready for each other when we get lost in God. We still have our judgments, our hurts, and fears. That person is skinny. That one is fat. That one looks mean. On and on and on go our judgments. And the little boys and girls in us just want to sing and dance.

Sita Ram. Sita Ram. Sita Ram.

And maybe, just maybe, our task in this world is to let those little boys and girls out and protect them. Yes, we must protect them because there are bad people in this world. And even most of the good people are not ready for the outpouring of God's love. It is too frightening. God's love bypasses everything we think we know. Our most intricate beliefs get stepped on as we dance and sing. We do not need our beliefs. We only need to greet our little boys and little girls.

Radhe. Radhe. Radhe. Radhe Govinda.

I am convinced utterly and totally that God is seeking to connect with my little boy. I am further convinced that it is only my little boy who can connect totally with God. This little boy connects with God in Stillness. Then he looks out with quiet eyes. But he wants to sing and dance. He knows balance is everything, for while he is unwise in the ways of the world, he is wise in the ways of God. Stillness is good, but so is singing and dancing.

Govinda Jaya Jaya.

But here is the mystery, the paradox. To sing and dance, we must forget who we think we are. That is true. But at the same time we must be strongly rooted in who we think we are. How else can I put it? We, our older selves, cannot be frightened. We must be strong. Otherwise we will forever repress our little boys and girls because these inner children, in their utter disregard of our fears, are terrifying. They will take us into a flow of love so strong that it is incomprehensible. But then something wonderful happens. We find out who we really are.

Om Shanti Shanti Shanti.

So, boys and girls—Sing. Dance. Laugh and be happy. For there we will find God. Sing loud and clap your hands. Or sing in a whisper and dance inside. God does not care!

Blessings,
    John Conley

Questioner: Baba Ram Jahn, explain Om to me.

Baba Ram Jahn: Ah, yes, Om. It is a word I used often as a child. For example, when my sister did something bad, I would say "Om! I'm going to tell Mom!"

Questioner: No, no. Baba Ram. I mean Om, the powerful Sanskrit mantra.

Baba Ram Jahn: Why, child, so do I. You see, I said Om several times a day as a child. By the time I was twelve I had said Om hundreds, if not thousands of times. It exerted its power over me, even though I did not know what it meant.

Questioner: But how can that be? Is Om that powerful?

Baba Ram Jahn: Not necessarily, daughter. It had to do more with my sister. She was always getting in trouble. And I was always saying, "Om! I'm going to tell on you." I also learned breath control, I might add, from running from her. Never underestimate the spiritual power of an angry sister, nor the scared and sacred power of Om.

March 4

Dear Friends,

    I want love to be easy.

    I talk about how God is love. I talk about the divine flow of love and how I want to hug everyone I meet and shout, "I love you." I talk about chanting the names of God and how my spirit reaches out to God. I talk about how I see God in the eyes of my friends. I talk about how I see God in the beauty of a woman. I talk about how I smell God in the dewed sweetness of a rose. I talk about how I taste God in the nectar of a pear. I have said that we are the nectar of God tasting ourselves.

    There are times I see God in suffering. I see God peeking out from eyes full of pain as an old woman tells me her son never comes to visit her. "He was going to come visit me on my birthday, but he had a cold. He is so busy. He wears himself out." Yes, I see God winking at me from her wrinkled face. And God is saying to me, "There is more here than you know."

    I see God in the face of the man who has no eyes, just sockets. He has no money to buy glass eyes. And he does not care what I think. His suffering has moved him beyond caring about trivial things. And he stares at me with scarred sockets and as I wonder what his eyes looked like, God stares at me and says, "Yes, John, even here there is more than you know."

    I see God in the hands of a man who has no fingers, just stumps. Did he say he lost them to a saw in a lumber mill? I don't remember. My mind was a little numb as I watched him use his stumps to scratch a match across a brick fireplace. He lit a cigarette then and inhaled deeply, as though meditating. His tee-shirt was dirty with catsup stains and God knows what else. His trailer home stunk and I could barely stand to be there. The smell twisted my stomach. He was ugly too, with rotten teeth, a scraggly beard, and uncombed hair. Yet, God winked at me and said, "I love this man, John. There is more here than you understand."

So, I sing my chants. I do my meditations, sometimes for many hours a day. I read ponderous books about the meaning of life. I smile and twinkle. And I feel happy because God is winking at me. Underneath all the suffering—and I see more of it than most, and less of it than many—I see the glory of God. I see what I call Stillness. I feel blessed.

I want love to be easy.

But love is not always easy. You see, sometimes my love is nothing but words. Sometimes it is just about feeling good. I can cope with the suffering of strangers. I can walk away from them. It is my work to serve them. But at the end of the day, I leave them. Many I never see again.

But when a loved one suffers, I want to hide. I want to run. I want to say, "How can I help you when I am so tired?" I think of all the times I have been used. I think of all the times I have been hurt. I think of all the things that could go wrong. I do not want to love if it means self-sacrifice. I do not want to love if it means taking risks.

I do not want to see the hurt in your eyes. I do not want to see the fear in your eyes, or the trembling in your hands. I do not want to tell you that I want to hold you and make everything better. I do not want to tell you I want to wave my magic wand and make all your hurt go away. It doesn't work that way. No, it's not that easy.

I want to run. Instead I take a step forward and then another. I may walk forward fearfully, but I walk nevertheless. And other than give you the precious gift of my time, there is not much I can give you, for I know so little. I know how to be still and I can share that with you. But I do not have answers.

And it's not easy because I cannot detach myself from your pain. I am not some all wise and powerful guru. I am just me. I am not even a mystic; or if I am, then I am a poor one. Mystical insights about illusion and detachment are wonderful until it's someone you love. My guess is that our insights often sadden God.

I think maybe the only insight we have that God takes seriously is the one that says, "Blunder forth and do your best to love." So, perhaps, no matter how frightened and confused we get, no matter how cowardly we feel, we can wink at each other and say, "There is more here than you understand."

Blessings,
    John Conley

Questioner: Baba Ram Jahn, I have made an amazing discovery.

Baba Ram Jahn: And what is that, child?

Questioner: Cows, Baba Ram Jahn, cows. Cows chant all day long, Moo. Moo. Moo. This is cow language for Oom. Oom. Oom. I know they are saying it backwards, but I may be able to teach them to say it forwards.

Baba Ram Jahn: That is very interesting, daughter.

Questioner: I have therefore decided, Father, to be a cowboy, so that I too may become enlightened.

Baba Ram Jahn: I am not quite sure what to say.

Questioner: Of course, I will need a horse first, and a saddle. Some boots. A barn to stable the horse. And I suppose we should get some cows. I think, Father, enlightenment can be very expensive and the path may ask much of us.

Baba Ram Jahn: I think, daughter, the path seems to be asking much of me!

March 11

Dear Friends,

Our minds can be like a wild mare, unfettered and free, as she gallops over the high grass. This is a delight. We can gallop across undiscovered plateaus of creativity and drink from mountain streams knowledge. But all too often, our minds can be like a rat, digging through the garbage and grunting with glee at every little nasty piece of trash. This is pain. Our rat minds nibble and chew at our peace, never giving us rest.

If our minds can cause us so much pain, what are we to do? We have all heard that it is not the reality of the outer world that causes us pain; rather, it is the reality of the inner world that causes us pain. It is our interpretation of events that causes pain. So how do we learn to reinterpret our experience?

For me there is only one way to reinterpret my experience and that is to enter into Stillness. And this is what I have learned about Stillness. It is there always, just underneath the chatter of our minds. It never goes anywhere or does anything. It is simply there. When our minds are quiet and our hearts still, we need no longer seek; for we have found that which was never lost—joy. I have experienced that joy, and with each day it grows. Stillness transforms my view of myself and my world. In Stillness, I am a new man. And I did nothing to make this happen.

"But is that true?" I ask myself. "Did I do nothing?" I think about my answer. On one hand, it is true. I have done nothing to become still. It is happening. I do not know why. It is what my mother called grace. On the other hand, I have worked hard. I focus on

Stillness every single day and I have for several years. I focus on Stillness when my mind screams with boredom. I focus on Stillness when I feel tired. I focus on Stillness when I feel lonely. Also, I have become watchful, like a scout in enemy territory. I have trained myself to become aware of the flow of my thoughts and feelings. When anger arises, or jealousy, or resentment, I know it. It is as though I am watching myself move slowly in a dream. And as I watch, I have time—not always!—to say, "This is not who I am."

My whole life has become a meditation. And it has required discipline, perseverance, and watchfulness; for otherwise I fear I will slip back into my old ways. In truth, this has been a long, hard journey. As meditation has become more central in my life, I have had to face my fears, my ignorance, and my pride. I have faced those aspects of myself I found most loathsome. All of these hidden ghosts came up as I reached for Stillness. It is as though Stillness intentionally brought up all my secrets to be healed. And I must heal them, or I cannot go deeper into Stillness. This journey is not always easy!

For me, this has been the most surprising step of my journey. I sought bliss, and instead I found myself, with all my pain. I sought knowledge, and again I found myself. I sought transcendence and when I found it, I was waiting for myself. I felt lonely, frightened, and confused. I stood in my own path and blocked myself. And I would not move until I found healing. No matter how hard I tried to ignore myself, to overcome myself, I could not. I could not progress on my spiritual journey until I dealt with my human journey. I could not take one step until I learned compassion for that most unlovable man called John.

It is as though we are the farmers of our own souls. God provides the sun, the earth and the rain. But we raggedy, old farmers have to sow the crops, hoe them, defend them against predators, harvest them, and store them in a safe place for winter. And as the farmer becomes one with the land, so we must become one with Stillness. We become Stillness by focusing on it. We focus on Stillness by digging in the dirt of life, and from that springs forth a bountiful harvest.

The pursuit of Stillness is a lifelong journey. I believe we must seek this Stillness with all our strength; and as we do, our whole life will find healing, for that which we seek is the balm for that which we flee. In Stillness we can find healing. And then even the most mundane tasks will take on a new freshness, like a field of red clover, kissed with the morning dew and caressed by the sun. We must pursue Stillness as we would a lover, one for whom we would give anything to share even a moment in her presence.

Our coming into joy is inevitable. I believe in grace. I believe it is our fate to awaken. But the path is arduous. And there are many pitfalls. So we must be diligent. We must be fearless. We must be watchful. We must cast our gaze on the horizon and step into the unknown. And there we will find that which was never lost.

Blessings,
    John Conley

Letters to My Friends

Questioner: Baba Ram Jahn, sometimes I get tired of being spiritual. It is all so serious. I want to play and be silly. Baba, would you quit making faces at me!

Baba Ram Jahn: Yes, sorry, child. You were saying?

Questioner: I want to play, to sing, and to dance. I am always meditating and reading big books with big words. Baba! What are you doing? How can you listen to me and do cartwheels at the same time? You will hurt yourself!

Baba Ram Jahn: You are right. You said something about being silly?

Questioner: Yes, Baba, I did. But you keep acting silly. So how can I think?

Baba Ram Jahn: You are right, my daughter. I am sure God sends silly people to hell. It is a good thing I am always serious.

Questioner: I am being serious, Baba!

Baba Ram Jahn: You are being serious about being silly? Isn't that just a bit silly?

Questioner: Yes, Baba! Now I see. When I am serious, I am being silly. Therefore, when I am playing, I am serious. I feel better now. I think I will be silly and read a long, boring book on theology. It is all one.

Baba Ram Jahn: Seriously? Did I say that? What I teach never ceases to amaze me.

March 17

Dear Friends,

Once, not too long ago, in a land far away, there was a young man named Won, and he wanted to find God. He set out from his home and headed to Japan. There he studied with the masters of Zen. He learned to breathe, to simply breathe and empty his mind. Soon, he could sit for hours, and then for days. After several years, he said to himself, "I have not found God. I have learned many wondrous things, but I have not found what I seek"

Won left Japan and traveled to China. There he studied with the great masters of the Tao. He learned to let life flow and he learned to flow with life. He studied for many years in China, and even the emperor heard of his wisdom. Won would say to those who came to see him, "That which can be spoken is not that which we seek." And then he would laugh. He became known as the laughing monk. But one day Won said to himself, "Still I do not know God." Soon afterward, he left for India.

There he studied with holy men of the forest, he learned about chakras and kundalini. He practiced Hatha Yoga and studied the Bhagavad-Gita. He learned many mantras. He learned about cleansing rituals. And he learned about karma. He practiced breath control, which the holy men called pranayama. And he sang the names of God. Won, whose raven hair had now turned to the color of slate, soon became known as a miracle worker and a healer. Even the creatures of the forest came to him for healing. But one day, Won said to himself, "I have learned many wonderful things. But still I have not found God."

He left India and headed to Persia. There he learned about

Allah and the Koran. From his Muslim friends, he learned about devoting his will to God. He prayed and danced and danced and prayed. He read the poetry of the Muslim mystics, and found great joy in the words. But still he said to himself, "I do not know God. What am I to do?"

Now, with a cane to aid him, he traveled to Jerusalem. And there he studied the ancient Hebrew texts. He partook in ecstatic prayer with the mystics of the deserts. He read the psalms and marveled at their beauty. He celebrated the Passover. He soaked in the wisdom of Abraham. But still he said to himself, "I do not know God. I cannot find God in the words."

His hair now the color of snow, he traveled to Rome. He learned about Jesus. He learned about the miracle of the resurrection. He learned about love. He learned about many mansions in heaven. He learned about asking for forgiveness. And he learned about service to others. But still, at last, he said to himself, "I do not know God. The words obscure my sight."

He turned around and headed for his home, many, many leagues away. As he walked, he mused to himself, "The older I get, the less I know. I thought that I was supposed to get wiser as I grew older. But I just seem to know less and less. Everyone else seems to know the truth. I alone seem uncertain."

He sat down on a rock at the foot of a mountain to rest, and continued thinking. "There are so many beliefs, so many rituals, so many thoughts, and they all seem as smoke to me. Yet many of those who follow these beliefs, believe them strongly. But for me, the slightest wind of my mind disperses them. None calls to me. All these beliefs seem like a man clutching at a straw while drowning in a river. And all the while, the man screams that he has found a mighty ship in which to sail to God."

John C. Conley

"Am I arrogant in my ignorance? Am I proud of being lost? Yet I cannot embrace any of these beliefs. They seem to ask me to believe too much about too much." Won felt sad. He wanted to believe, but he could not. The words of all that he had learned seemed to hide God. Slowly Won gathered his strength and pushed himself up from the rock upon which he sat.

As he traveled, as was his custom, he tended to the sick when he entered the villages along his way. He told stories of his travels and he laughed and joked. If he had two apples, he gave one away. If he had a loaf a bread, he shared it. He had a smile for everyone he met. But he had not found God.

Won was very old now. He moved slowly. He had an ache in his belly that he knew must be some sickness. One day, he awoke in the morning and he simply could not get up. "My time has come," he thought. "I am dying and I have not found God. I can only hope God finds me." And with that thought, he died.

The ravens and the ants, the snakes and the gophers all gathered around Won. As one, they lifted him and carried him to heaven and set him by a great lake. There Won awoke as from a deep sleep. He arose and walked along a broad path in a meadow painted with daffodils and daisies. On either side of the path stood many, many people. He recognized these people from his journeys! They waved at him and smiled at him. There was the young man who had died of an arrow wound in battle. Won had tried to help, but ended doing nothing more than holding his hand as he died. And there was the little girl with whom he had once shared an apple. There were Muslims, Hindus, Jews, Christians, and Buddhists, all together, all smiling and waving at him. Perplexed, but happy to see these wonderful people from his life on earth, Won walked on until he came to the end of the path.

Letters to My Friends

A small boy stood before him. Won recognized the boy. And the boy said, "Are you happy now Won? You have found me."

"Found you? But you are the boy I met in the village near the sea. Your mother had died, and I found you alone and deserted in the streets. I gave you my robe to keep you warm. But you died in the night. I grieved for you. But, forgive me, I have not been looking for you."

"Do you not see, even now, my child?" said the boy. "I am God. When you loved me, you loved God. When you fed me, you fed God. When you held me and comforted me, you held and comforted God."

"But I did not know you! I believed nothing. There were days I did not even believe in love. All the words left me feeling empty and alone. I could not find God in them."

"Oh, but Won, I tried to tell you again and again, life is about who you love, not what you know. And you, Won, loved greatly." And with that the little boy laughed and threw himself in the arms of Won.

Blessings,
    John Conley

Questioner: Father, I met an astrologer, and she told me I am an Aries. She said I have planets in different houses. These planets affect how I act.

Baba Ram Jahn: No, no, daughter. You misunderstood her. She said you have houseplants and these houseplants affect your life. For example, when you walk into a room and see a vase of jasmine, your heart sings.

Questioner: No, Master, she said this had something to do with the stars.

Baba Ram Jahn: Do you mean to tell me that there are houseplants on the stars?

Questioner: It is a wondrous universe in which we live, Baba. Do you see the stars as they twinkle at us? Do you see how they sway? The stars rejoice with us and dance for joy.

About the Author

Raised in a small Oregon logging town where fighting, drinking, and God were the main entertainment, John had his first introduction to fighting and God in Sunday school. Drinking came later. Ever since those Sunday school days, he has argued endlessly with himself about what God is. And when he gets tired of arguing with himself, he argues with God. John began meditating when he was eighteen years old to impress his girlfriend. She found another boyfriend, but John, broken-hearted, continued to meditate, after punching his opposition in the nose.

For many years John had a somewhat nomadic life. Hippie, soldier, commercial fisherman, student, drunk, newspaper reporter, freelance writer, insurance salesman, tree trimmer, cook, and construction worker were but a few of the jobs he tried. But throughout them all, he meditated.

And he continued to argue with God. Now he, John, not God, thinks he has something worthwhile to share about meditation, life, and how to be, if not happy, less miserable. Does he? Maybe, maybe not. You be the judge.

When he is not meditating or saving the world, John likes to walk in the woods near his home. He likes to play guitar and sing. He likes to dance like a wild man. And he likes to hug. He loves his family and his friends. He loves the two cats and the woman who let him live in their house. And whenever he thinks he is enlightened, he remembers how he often wants to yell at his neighbor when her dogs bark and bark and bark at nothing. Nothing? Perhaps they are Buddhist dogs and they are chanting *Om Mani Peme Hung* in dogese?

Order Information

Books can be ordered through:

www.mondaynightmeditation.com

Letters to My Friends can also be ordered through bookstores worldwide.

ISBN 978-0-9727531-4-2